D1630550

EUROPEAN SCULPTURE
from Romanesque to Rodin

EUROPEAN SCULPTURE
from Romanesque to Rodin

H. D. MOLESWORTH

in collaboration with

P. CANNON BROOKES

THAMES AND HUDSON
LONDON

This book is sold subject to the condition that it shall not, by way of trade, be lent, re-sold, hired out, or otherwise disposed of without the publisher's consent, in any form of binding or cover other than that in which it is published.

© THAMES AND HUDSON 1965
PRINTED IN ITALY BY AMILCARE PIZZI MILAN

Contents

Preface   7

Introduction   9

I   MEDIEVAL SCULPTURE IN THE NORTH

The Romanesque   19

Early Gothic   47

Mid Gothic   60

Late Gothic   70

II ITALIAN SCULPTURE

The Trecento   97

The Quattrocento   105

High Renaissance and Mannerism   146

Baroque and Rococo   171

III THE BEGINNINGS OF MODERN SCULPTURE

The Mid Sixteenth to Mid Seventeenth Centuries   195

The Mid Seventeenth to Eighteenth Centuries   231

The Nineteenth Century   259

Select Bibliography   269

List of Illustrations   277

Index   286

Preface

To attempt to record in detail the sculpture of nearly one thousand years within the scope of one volume would manifestly be to attempt the impossible; a recital of the published names alone would occupy more space. In this book we have therefore chosen to provide a series of essays on the background to the principal schools and periods, and in the main it has been left to the illustrations themselves to convey the general evolution of the art.

The book has been divided for convenience into three sections: first, medieval sculpture from the eleventh to the sixteenth centuries, in which we are mainly concerned with the North.

Second, Italian sculpture, in which Italian works of the Gothic period, the Renaissance and later centuries are seen as a sequence which, however influential on the rest of Europe, remains spiritually somewhat apart.

Third, sculpture from the sixteenth to the nineteenth centuries. By the beginning of this period the foundations of modern Europe, political, social and intellectual, had been laid, and to these modern conditions the sculptures conform. The fundamental approach changes but little until the advent of contemporary styles.

The first and third of these sections are largely the work of H. D. Molesworth, the second of P. Cannon Brookes.

Though the specialist may offer objections to this broad and arbitrary division, we feel that for the reader seeking an introduction to the art it affords a useful and reasonably valid classification, and a basis for more detailed study of the contribution of individual artists and of the complex interplay and ramifications of the various national schools.

1 Supporting figures on a central door-post from Beaulieu, France. Stone, dating from the early twelfth century.

Introduction

In this book we shall be looking at European sculpture from the twelfth century to the beginning of contemporary styles in the nineteenth century. Apart from a short period at the beginning, we find above all the revival of a classical heritage, with all that this implies in intellectual approach and presentation. The concentration is on a naturalistic treatment of the human body as the vehicle for ideas, whether secular or religious, intellectual or imaginative. Only in the sculpture of the extreme north, in Scandinavia and the Anglo-Saxon areas, up to the eleventh or twelfth centuries, did any alternative approach even suggest itself until the abstract forms of the mid-twentieth century.

Throughout these centuries of classical revival, Europe has been a Christian world, and sculpture has played a major part in the promulgation of its legends and beliefs. Indeed, for the first centuries of our period religious sculpture is almost the only sculpture, and even later, when monuments or decorative works become more general, they are inevitably conditioned by the Christian attitude. Thus at the outset we find a paradoxical situation, in which an art ultimately founded upon that of a pagan-humanist civilization is pressed into the service of ideals and doctrines directed to a negation of the flesh.

René Huyghe draws attention to a basic dichotomy when he writes that there are 'two essential impulses received by Europe—Platonism, which gives primacy to the idea, and Aristotelianism, which gives its experimental knowledge.' More specifically, he speaks of the two aesthetic ideals: that of 'ideal beauty, conceived and imposed by the mind', the Platonic approach, and 'realistic truth, which has accepted the dictation by the eye', which is

Aristotelian. Something of both these approaches is inherent in all sculpture. But in broad outline—and in this review we are more concerned to obtain an overall perspective than to deal with exceptions—the Mediterranean areas have been chiefly moved by the senses, while in the Northern countries the disciplines imposed by the mind have had the greater influence.

Tradition—or at least a century of common practice—has further divided the European sculptural heritage into such broad categories as Romanesque, Gothic, Renaissance, Baroque, and so on. These divisions are valid and there seems no reason to avoid them. But if what we mean by these terms can usually be recognized visually even by the layman, a verbal definition is quite another matter. The *Oxford English Dictionary*, for example, in a column some six inches deep devoted to 'Romanesque', has as its most comprehensive entry—'architecture'—only the following: 'Prevalent in, or distinctive to buildings erected in Romanised Europe between the close of the Classical period and the rise of Gothic architecture'. Under 'painting' there appears a most curious entry supported by the authority of '1842. Brande Dict. Sci.', which reads: 'Romanesque—in historical painting, it consists in the choice of a fanciful subject, rather than one founded on fact.' This at least tells us that the term was used in 1819. 'Gothic', accorded a column-and-a-half, has 'Belonging to, or characteristic of, the Middle Ages; medieval, "romantic" as opposed to classical [which is just what it was to Walter Scott, though it is perhaps not so for us today]. In early use, chiefly with reprobation.'

These entries are not quoted in order to call the Dictionary into question, but to emphasize that these divisions in visual art are best accepted *visually*, and that they evade precise definition.

To complicate classification still further: elements of most styles are found at all times, and at transitional periods where there is an overlap it can become a point of argument as to whether the work belongs to one category or another. In this book the presentation of the various styles has therefore been left largely to the illustrations, while in the text we seek mainly to outline the background of the periods, and to offer some account of the complex circumstances—the economic and political backgrounds, the aims and tastes of patrons and artists—which have made their contribution to the evolution of sculpture.

The principal changes which have taken place over the past thousand years are introduced by the group of illustrations which follows. To make comparison easier the same subject, the caryatid, has been chosen in each case. (The term caryatid is used in its popular sense, for a supporting figure of either sex.) At any period the sight of the labouring man bearing his burden is a significant subject, one common to everybody's everyday experience, and it is also one which, by its very modesty, imposes no particular style on the artist.

There is obviously no more doctrinal importance in a caryatid on a building or a pulpit than there is in any poor old man —or a young one for that matter—carrying a burden on his shoulders: and yet the subject is so intensely part of life and touches a nerve so universal that artists at all periods have been profoundly struck by it. The subject recurs again and again, as the caryatid allows the sculptor to express the burden of humanity as he sees it. The Romanesque mystic created a strange, contorted, elongated, robed, priestly figure (*Ill.* 1), while for a later, more practical, medieval sculptor the burden is carried by a round-shouldered and impoverished peasant (*Ill.* 2); he is unable to bear arms for war, and obviously lacks the intellectual equipment to become a clerk of the Church. In the late Gothic the sculptor Adam Krafft produced a self-portrait (*Ill.* 3). The Renaissance sculptors and Mannerists brought intellectual detachment as well as beauty to their subjects (*Ill.* 4). In the eighteenth century Permoser in the Zwinger chose a jolly, youthful Bacchus accompanied by an equally jolly old faun to bear the burdens of the world, while in Prague the sculptor M. B. Braun shows

2,3 Supporting figures: *left*, from the base of a niche, Amiens Cathedral, France, mid thirteenth century; *right*, in the form of a self-portrait by Adam Krafft, Sebaldskirche, Nuremberg, late fifteenth century.

the same type as Atlas (*Ill.* 5). Just as significant in this series are the supporters of the early Epstein (*Ill.* 6), products of the modern gymnasium and the sportsfield.

Apart from certain objects produced as works of beauty in their own right, particularly at the Renaissance and in the eighteenth century, and purely decorative carvings—the animals and foliage on capitals, bandings, or scrollwork, which tend to fall under the slightly derogatory term of 'carving'—the greater part of European sculpture was intended primarily to fulfil a particular function as a religious icon, or as a personal or public monument.

In the early part of our period religious sculpture is predominant, but later, with the iconoclasm of the various reforming movements, it gives place to the personal tomb or monument,

12

to the portrait, and to decorative or architectural works. The profound influence of function upon style emerges extremely clearly. In religious sculptures we have a particularly good example. The intellectual-mystical beliefs of the Romanesque artists seem to demand a quite different style of handling from the emotional mysticism of the seventeenth century, and the high idealism of Gothic could not be expressed with the joyous freedom of Rococo. Indeed, whatever the predominant theological approach of any period, it is always reflected in the handling of the sculptures. This influence may be said to be two-way, for if current theology affected the style of the sculptures, the images in turn served to create a new image of God and his saints for succeeding generations.

The classical-Jewish inheritance in which man is regarded as fashioned in the likeness of God restricts representations of the deity to the human form—in this unlike the deities of other

4,5,6 Supporting figures by, *from left to right*, Jean Goujon, mid sixteenth century; M. B. Braun, early eighteenth century; and Jacob Epstein, early twentieth century.

groups, which are represented with all the intricacies that mystery, imagination and abstract form can give them. Even so, attitudes towards the Christian God, to Christ, the Virgin and the saints have changed, and at different times they have assumed different aspects. Four representations of Christ, below (*Ills.* 7 to 10), speak for themselves. If the caryatids illustrated changes in style for a secular subject, these show how the sculptor's conception of a sacred subject, too, changes with the period.

The monument did not begin to be important until the thirteenth century, but from then on it became as capable as religious sculpture of reflecting its time, and indeed of affecting style. Its importance increased after the iconoclastic reformations of the sixteenth century. The change of status is immediately apparent if we compare the simple effigy of a knight in armour (*Ill.* 12) with the monument to General Wolfe in Westminster Abbey (*Ill.* 11). In the latter the scene is conducted as though

7,8 Head of Christ, *left*, from a capital at Plaimpied, France, twelfth century; and *right*, from the West Porch of Ulm Cathedral, Germany, mid fifteenth century.

it were the final act in a classical drama. The deceased is portrayed making an address, doubtless in exquisitely polished prose or verse, lying unclad on a camp bed, while his attendant officers look as though they have only just failed to conform to the period conceit of taking time off to dress up in what a lively historical imagination regarded as the costume of high-ranking Romans. In these two contrasting presentations is caught the whole atmosphere of the Gothic and the eighteenth century respectively.

The monuments of the two Princes of the Church from the same cathedral at Mainz (*Ills*. 13, 14) similarly reflect the late fifteenth and late seventeenth centuries in Germany. The first approaches portraiture and is a down-to-earth statement of fact consistent with a sixteenth century burgher attitude of mind. But in the second monument (*Ill*. 14), executed some two hundred years later, the princely Archbishop is portrayed in a mixture of sumptuous dishabille and Church regalia, reclining on a mat

9,10 Head of Christ, *left*, from the Florence *Pietà* by Michelangelo, marble, sixteenth century; and *right*, from the Entombment by Gregorio Fernández, Valladolid, Spain, painted wood, late sixteenth century.

11 Joseph Wilton: Monument to General Wolfe in Westminster Abbey, London. Marble, dating from 1772.

—something he would certainly never have done in life. He is attended by a naked child who sportively holds up a book which might quite as well be secular as religious from the expression of the deceased. The underlying ideas of life and art are so astonishingly different that it is hard to imagine that both were created in the same country and for the same church, and that they are merely separated by a few generations of change in human thought. Each is imbued with the social codes, the teachings and the emotions of its own time, and expresses them in a synthesis which would be almost impossible except to the visual arts.

12 Effigy of a knight from Dorchester Abbey, Oxfordshire. Stone, c.1300.

13 Monument to the Prince-Bishop
Dieter von Isenburg, d. 1482, in
Mainz Cathedral, Germany. Stone,
late fifteenth century.

14 Monument to the Prince-Bishop
Franz von Ingelheim in Mainz Cathedral. Marble, late seventeenth century.

15 The Adoration of the Magi. Whalebone, 14 in. high. Probably English work of the twelfth century.

MEDIEVAL SCULPTURE IN THE NORTH

The Romanesque

Apart from the geographically limited though very remarkable development of the Celtic northern crosses or the Scandinavian carvings and doorways (*Ill.* 16), European sculpture on a monumental scale was desultory to say the least for the five or six centuries after the collapse of Rome. It was also generally somewhat childish in both conception and execution. Occasionally there is a fine relief, or a tomb makes its mark on a church floor in memory of some soldier or prelate. Occasionally there is decorative banding, or panels with reliefs such as this from Monreale (*Ill.* 17); sometimes there are even carved pulpits or more ambitious objects such as the great bronze doors and fonts or the column of Bernward at Hildesheim or the stuccos at Cividale. Here and there, particularly in the Italian peninsula where the mass of classical remains must have served as a continual reminder that sculpture had once flourished, an enthusiast was stirred to try his hand. But there is nowhere work of any real aesthetic distinction—except in the ivories, and to a lesser extent in the metalwork.

What occurs in these, then, is of fundamental importance, for they represent the continuation of sculpture, right through from classical times. It is often contended that sculpture died out as an art with the Dark Ages and Byzantine iconoclasm, to be revived *de novo* in the twelfth century. But this is not the case. Sculpture merely changed its scale, and, as we need not be afraid to stress, scale is not necessarily significant in the expression of stylistic developments.

Throughout the centuries a wide variety of concurrent styles were manifest in the ivories, and these styles were continued in the larger-scale works of the twelfth century renaissance. Indeed, the essentials of Romanesque sculpture of 1100 are already present in works such as the ivory Crucifix of S. Isidoro (*Ill.* 18) which dates from before 1063. To account for this wide variety of styles we have only to recall that in the scattered churches and abbeys, as in the earlier court and monastic workshops, individuality could still flourish, and that there was a wide range of sources from which ideas could be taken. There was little prejudice in the minds of the carvers, and examples from almost any period were drawn upon with lively interest. Not until the ecclesiastical regimentation of the thirteenth century did real uniformity begin to obtain.

The superb whalebone Madonna and Child (*Ill.* 15) has been chosen as the first illustration of Romanesque sculpture not only

16 (*left*) Detail of the doorway, church at Urnes, Norway. Mid eleventh century.

17 (*right*) Adam and Eve, panel from the West Door, Monreale Cathedral. Bronze, eleventh century.

18 Crucifix of San Isidoro.
Ivory, mid eleventh century.

because the quality is beyond compare, but because in every
detail, from the animals to the drapery and features, she seems
to represent the time ... not least, perhaps, in the fact that
scholars have disagreed for nearly a century about her origin, and
even date. If a claim can be made for England, it is only one
of many, and bears witness to the fact that the early medieval
world was indeed a world, albeit a warring one, rather than a
collection of nations with frontiers and national prejudices. Whatever their disagreements, the ruling houses were closely inter-
woven by marriage, and the whole of day-to-day feudal society
depended from them when it did not depend from the Church,
which was equally international. Prelates and monks of all
regions from Armenia to Northern England might journey to

21

and fro and take up appointments anywhere. Pilgrims, too, travelled widely, so that within the admittedly limited range of practical demand, artistic ideas and small transportable works of art went from one area to another, and wherever they went they exercized their influence.

It was from these widely diverse sources that the new monumental Romanesque sculptures arose.

Why and how did this revival of monumental sculpture take place? The answer is that we do not know. But if it is not known exactly why or how the movement started, at least we know when and where.

In a brief account such as this any attempt to adjudicate between the claims of one church or another to be the first would be out of place. In any case, the lead can only be a matter of a few years, and it is enough for our purposes to accept that the whole movement began in the two decades immediately before and after 1100, on a line drawn from Northern Spain to Southern France and Northern Italy, and that within one generation it had spread over virtually the whole of Europe. The interplay of medieval history is highly complicated, and it is perhaps enough here to say that this sculptural revival appears at the moment when the Church finally emerges triumphant from the age-old struggle with the Empire for temporal as well as spiritual domination. The great victory of Canossa was in 1077, and the concluding act of this drama, the Concordat of Worms, took place in 1122. Between these years, Romanesque sculpture evolved.

All the new works appear under ecclesiastical auspices and upon ecclesiastical property, and are therefore as intimately bound up with the political and temporal circumstances of the Church as with the spiritual and philosophical changes.

With the Crusades abroad and the active proselytization at home, the Church's militant activities were everywhere to the fore. Within the Church, if the cultured humanist traditions of the eleventh century still prevailed in many high places, the ascetic, reforming activities of men like Arnold of Brescia and St Bernard were beginning to make great headway in the ideals if not always the practices of churchmen. Both types of outlook were important for sculpture, since although the reformed ideas did not dominate the scene immediately, their effect became paramount later on. Those who promoted the beginnings of monumental sculpture within the Church were not, of course, the reformers who were hostile, but men brought up in the highly-civilized tradition of monastic and university learning of the previous century. They were the heirs of and successors to the scholastic philosophers and to contemplative monasticism, with a background of intellectualism, classical learning, grammar and dialectic.

Predictably enough, then, Romanesque sculpture is at first a somewhat refined art, in which aesthetics of line and form take precedence over any straightforward statement of the subject, just as in the universities the catena of logical argument must have given as much pleasure to a contemporary intellectual as the accepted premise or conclusion. A style of this kind was in full accord with the mystical tenets of the day, and indeed, with the current feudalism, which was still a formal pattern from which all social order depended, rather than the emotional chivalric creed that it was later to become, and that Gothic sculpture was to express.

The historical background also explains why we find the first sculptures chiefly along the main pilgrimage routes. For the medieval man pilgrimage to worship at a shrine of relics was one of the passports to heaven and a way of redeeming sin. The greatest pilgrimage of all was naturally to the Holy Land, but where this was impossible pilgrimages were made to Rome or to St James at Compostella. Since the Moors were occupying the Peninsula, a visit there was no doubt akin to a visit to the front line. The custom was exploited, and a number of centres

19 Christ in Majesty, from the Tympanum of St Foy, Conques, France. Stone, early twelfth century.

grew up along the pilgrimage roads with greater or lesser shrines and relics and attendant miracles, doubtless encouraged by a mixture of genuine piety and business acumen. The new carvings were designed to proclaim the Faith and at the same time to enhance the curiosity attraction. Indeed, by the 1120s there was almost a tourist guide to these pilgrimage centres.

As the whole idea of monumental sculpture had fallen into abeyance, on its revival neither artists nor patrons had such firm traditions or preconceived ideas as would have prevented them from picking and choosing and experimenting. This in fact they did, and one curious feature is that they seem to have been indifferent as to the date of the models from which they drew their ideas, as the illustrations which follow show.

Since they are the focal point of the new sculpture-complexes we will first mention the great figures of Christ in Majesty that appear on almost all the early tympani. These naturally differ slightly, but the general treatment is similar everywhere, and the figure at Conques (*Ill.* 19) is an excellent example. The inspiration seems to be graphic rather than plastic, and the formal stylization of the folds, leading up to the hieratic, staring face, are like a translation into stone of a painted or manuscript device. The manner serves to increase the spectator's feeling of awe.

The narrative scenes that appear in almost every complex are usually somewhat more straightforward and representational. In the most primitive of these the carvings are rather childish, but the better examples present lively bustling scenes of considerable vigour. The heads are usually egg-shaped and the eyes bulbous—sometimes pierced and filled with lead for greater effect. The drapery may consist of rather formal pleats. like that of the Christ-figures or be rendered by incised lines. In these scenes the reliefs on antique sarcophagi seem to have had some influence, and are perhaps responsible for the greater plasticity, as in the vigorous Doom which accompanies the Christ from Conques (*Ill.* 20).

20 Detail of the Last Judgment, from the Tympanum of St Foy, Conques, France. Stone, early twelfth century.

21 (*left*) St Andrew, from the cloister of St Pierre, Moissac, France. Stone, *c.* 1100. Half life-size.

22 (*right*) The Prophet Isaiah, from the Abbey Church of Souillac, France. Stone, early twelfth century. Approximately half life-size.

The sarcophagi also appear to have influenced the simpler, larger-scale figures of saints under arched niches, such as those at St Sernin at Toulouse and at Moissac (*Ill.* 21). The pattern for these saints has often been sought in manuscripts or even in consular ivories where the motif was common, but in this case close affinity with panels on late Gallo-Roman sarcophagi (now in the Musée des Augustins at Toulouse) seems to suggest that no further search is necessary.

But alongside these figures and scenes we find a whole group of figures totally different in conception and treatment. The Beaulieu doorpost (*Ill. 1*) is an example, but the prophets from Souillac (*Ill. 22*) are perhaps the finest expression of this departure. Here, suddenly, we find sculpture of the highest genius and individuality. In some ways these figures may be paralleled in the more fantastic manuscripts, yet as translated in the early twelfth century in the Languedoc they appear as the purely plastic creation of a great artist. The popularity of this style and its influence is shown by the persistence of the idiom—an almost dancing contortion, and especially the treatment of the beards—which continues even to Chartres (*Ill. 23*).

This dancing movement and stylized elongation is repeated in a number of other groups, such as the great tympanum at Autun

23 St John the Baptist, from the West Porch of Chartres Cathedral. Stone, later twelfth century.

24,25 Central doorposts from, *left*, St Pierre, Moissac, and *right*, the Abbey Church of Souillac. Both stone, early twelfth century.

(*Ill.* 30). This pays some tribute to the narrative school but is infinitely more refined, attenuated and elegant.

The same type of approach is to be found in the fabulous central doorpost at Moissac (*Ill.* 24), created from formal addorsed lions. In this extremely decorative conception Eastern influences, perhaps introduced through textiles, seem to be active. Possibly also owing a debt to textiles, though deriving from early sculpture forms, appear formulae like those of *Samson and*

26 Samson and the Lion, a stone capital from Anzy-le-Duc, France. Twelfth century.

27 The hunter roundel from St Gilles, France. Stone, second half of the twelfth century.

28 Christ Blessing and St Michael, walrus-ivory head of a tau cross. English, mid twelfth century. Height 2¼ in.

the Lion (*Ill. 26*). The somewhat later hunter from St Gilles (*Ill. 27*) almost certainly derives from a woven source.

It seems that the Saxon-Celtic interlaced ornament, rather than Alexandrian or Mediterranean models, contributed to the Souillac doorpost (*Ill. 25*), and comparison of the doorpost with the Gloucester candlestick or contemporary ivories is revealing. Similarly, juxtaposition of the ivory tau cross (*Ill. 28* above) and some of the capitals at Toulouse (*Ill. 29* below) given to the later part of the century establishes their interdependence and bears witness to the long persistence of this Northern tradition.

29 Capital from the Church of St Sernin, Toulouse, France. Stone, second half of the twelfth century.

30 Detail of the Last Judgment, from Autun Cathedral, France. Stone, mid twelfth century.

A blending of the graphic representational style and the style of the dancing prophet could account for the notable achievements in the second generation, like Vézelay, or above all Autun (*Ill.* 30), which, despite their dependence on the linear insistence of the drapery, are essentially plastic.

Unfortunately, as Romanesque moves on towards Gothic the fantasy disappears, and the drapery, becoming increasingly severe, seems more like a poor adaptation of classical models than the brilliant handling of an original motif. The novelty lies in sculpture's increasing association with, and sometimes even subservience to architecture. By the mid century, when the centre of interest has moved north to the Ile de France, this idiom has become more insistent in examples such as Bourges, St Denis or Chartres. The figure from Avallon (*Ill.* 31) is typical: the lines of the drapery have become almost another band of mouldings, blending into the new soaring architecture. The southern version of this development, which can be seen at St Gilles or St Trophime at Arles (*Ill* 32), is perhaps a little more classically sculptural: the whole approach is modified to accord with the Roman triumphal arch. In comparison with the Souillac figures the new sculpture is disappointing, but it was to loosen up again as full Gothic in the late twelfth and thirteenth century with excellent results.

So far all the examples we have chosen have been from France, and this reflects the vital importance of this region, and the range of styles which were concurrent in one generation and one area—even in one complex. Such a variety of styles side by side is a phenomenon not found again until centuries later.

Elsewhere in Europe, the revived sculpture shows an equal independence and variety of approach in the early decades of the century. In England the Chichester reliefs (*Ill.* 33) are most probably indigenous, and the same claim can be made for the whalebone Madonna mentioned earlier (*Ill.* 15). From Kilpeck in the west to the series of carved doorways in Yorkshire, many examples of the new movement remain *in situ*, though few are still in the same impressive condition as those at Malmesbury (*Ill.* 34).

In Spain complexes like Santo Domingo de Silos or Oviedo are early examples of the style, and many other places, culminating in the great Church of St James at Compostella, have later carvings of high quality. Here in Spain, in particular, the Romanesque persisted in the smaller wooden figures such as the Madonnas from Vich. In Germany, or rather in the Germanic territories, the movement was not so widespread, but the screen

31 (*left*) A Prophet from Avallon, France. Stone, mid twelfth century.

32 (*right*) Detail of the West Porch, St Trophime, Arles, France. Stone, mid twelfth century.

at Bamberg (*Ill. 35*) illustrates a handling of great imagination and quality.

In Italy the most notable early achievements are well represented by the carvings of the sculptor Wilgelmus at Modena (*Ill. 37*), which recall the narrative types of the contemporary Languedoc churches, though they are perhaps a little more robustly plastic as befits their Roman heritage. This is certainly

33 The Raising of Lazarus, Chichester Cathedral, England. Stone, twelfth century.

true of the great works of the later sculptor Antellami at Parma (*Ill.* 38), where the monumental representations of the months are outstanding. Throughout the Italian peninsula there are many carvings of the period, but the majority do not attain the quality of the southern French sculptures.

In this survey of the new sculpture we have so far left out one most important development: the decorative use of animals and, to a lesser extent, of foliage on the bandings and capitals. While elaborate formal patterns might be evolved, as in the

34 The Apostles, Malmesbury Abbey, England. Stone, mid twelfth century.

35 Detail from the Choir Screen, Bamberg Cathedral, Germany. Stone, early thirteenth century.

36 Beast from a frieze, Church of St Gilles, France. Stone, second half of the twelfth century.

lions at Moissac, the rendering is often very acutely observed, and is more naturalistic than the sculptures of human subjects. The splendid beast from St Gilles, above, is a striking example. The introduction of naturalistic animal motifs seems a deliberate

37 Wilgelmus: Scenes from the Creation. Modena Cathedral, Italy. Stone, eleventh to twelfth century.

38 B. Antellami: *December*, from the Labours of the Months, in the Baptistery of San Giovanni, Parma, Italy. Stone, late twelfth century. Half life-size.

concession to popular feeling in this highly intellectual opening period. It must have meant much to people living close to nature to see a rabbit or a partridge portrayed as they knew them in the fields. Even the bewildered, awestruck peasant could find something familiar and less menacing than the Dooms and devils appearing elsewhere.

PURPOSE AND PRESENTATION

With very few exceptions the new figure sculptures appear either on a monumental scale on the porches, or on a much smaller scale on the capitals. It is worth stressing this point, since it is important for the understanding of the beginnings of

Romanesque, and, indeed, of the development of sculpture through the next three or four centuries.

Contemporary documents reveal that there were at least two practical intentions behind the new movement, quite apart from any aesthetic purposes. The first was to provide propaganda for the Church and the Faith. The second, the continuation of an earlier use of art, was to stimulate the individual to contemplation. These purposes were fulfilled by the fronts and the capitals respectively, and explain the development of each.

In their scale and treatment the capital carvings are a logical continuation of the intimate, personal arts—the ivories or manuscripts which had always flourished in the monasteries and

39 The Third Mode of Music, on a capital from the Abbey of Cluny, France. Stone, eleventh to twelfth century.

40 Toothache and a thorn in the foot, depicted on capitals from Wells Cathedral, England. Stone, early thirteenth century.

had served as aids to private meditation. Whether in cloister or church, the capital is not readily seen and is scarcely an obvious propaganda platform; yet its very obscurity makes it specially suitable as an object of study for the contemplative who would search out the subject matter. Indeed the iconoclastic Cistercian critics complained that people could become so engrossed in the curious mythical scenes as to be distracted from the proper subjects of religious contemplation, and accordingly sought to curb the movement.

Fortunately they did not succeed, and there followed the development of sculpture on the capitals, later spreading to the bosses, misericords, screens and stalls. Freedom from the dogmatic needs of the façades allowed the sculptor a much more human approach, in which nature and even humour could play a part. For the next four hundred years the caps and jambs, the corbels and bosses become the home of mask and bird, beast and plant, with scenes—sometimes even ribald scenes—from the day to day life of the people (*Ill.* 40).

This popularization is perhaps less marked at the beginning, and such examples as the capitals from Cluny (*Ill.* 39) are an interesting witness to the remote, intellectual preoccupations of monastic life in the twelfth century. Among their subjects were the not unexpected personifications of the virtues, but they also included the winds, the rivers of Paradise, and the modes of music, subjects recondite enough to be well above the intellectual conceit of any passing villein and to show the type of public for which these works were carved, and that the interest was perhaps more in art than in the subject matter.

It was quite otherwise with the tympani. Here the new propagandists took over in earnest, as is apparent in both the subjects and the treatment. Moissac provides an admirable example. In the centre is Christ in Majesty as a dread, feudal overlord, attended by the apocalyptic ancients shown as a row of crowned figures carved at a fraction of the size of Christ

41 Temple of Parasurameswar, India, *c.* A.D. 750. Detail of the west façade of the tower.

42 The Tympanum of the Church of St Pierre at Moissac, France. Stone, c. 1100.

(*Ill*. 42). Here, indeed, is the Church triumphant over temporal power, or so it must have appeared to medieval man accustomed to the etiquettes of presentation. Next come doctrinal themes of a more immediately popular and moral turn, such as the spirited rendering of Dives and Lazarus to the right of the porch, and the judgment Doom. The warning for the rich doubtless served equally well as a palliative for the poor, and in the treatment of the devils, as at Conques (*Ill*. 20), there seems to be a deliberate attempt at humour to catch the popular fancy, though it has a considerably grimmer twist than that of the curious little chimerae on the capitals.

The siting of these carvings at the main entrance to the principal buildings expresses the determination that their lessons should not be lost upon the viewers. The Church was triumphant on earth and her doctrines were to prevail.

What gave rise to this conception of presenting a central scene surrounded by bands of decoration we do not know, but it is interesting to compare the earlier temple carving from India (*Ill.* 41) in which both organization and handling are rather similar. With the medieval movement to and from the Middle East, what more likely than that a traveller's description of such a temple should have come to the attention of a ready-witted priest or baron, who saw its potentialities for his own creed? Such an explanation would at least account for the remarkable fact that the Languedoc group, especially, is totally unlike any of the classical triumphal arches which were still extant in the area. However or whenever it was conceived and executed, the novel idea gave rise to a movement in sculpture over the succeeding centuries on a scale which the world had never seen before.

PATRONAGE

The realization of sculptures even on the comparatively small scale of Moissac must have called for a considerable feat of organization, practical, political and intellectual. In Professor Panofski's phrase, it needed 'the man whose prestige and initiative summons other men's work into being'. Then as now, public works were no doubt most often accomplished by the dynamism and energy of one dedicated individual. In the case of an innovation like Moissac in 1100, the initiator must have been powerful, courageous and imaginative. The medium was new, and to appreciate *de novo* what such an entrance would look like from the artist's description, then to arrange for the sculptor to realize his conception, and to carry along with him the ecclesiastical committees and the local populace represents an administrative achievement that is indeed amazing.

Curiously enough we know very little about the medieval patrons, and we should know even less were it not that Abbot Suger, the instigator of the rebuilding of St Denis in Paris, has

43 Christ in Majesty, from the Tympanum, Shobden, England. Stone, mid twelfth century.

left what is virtually an autobiography. Though this dates from some forty years later than Moissac, things can have changed very little at the time he was writing, in 1141. We find a truly remarkable mixture of piety and opportunism, attention to detail, faith, saintliness and downright business acumen, as he begged money, trampled on opposition and tradition alike, and bullied and cajoled kings and potentates for his ends. Myths, miracles, prayers and detailed supervision are all intermingled. Naturally religious justification is claimed for all of this, but at the same time, the whole work is so fired with the enthusiasm of the collector that however sincere the expressions of piety or justified the theological reasoning, they become almost hypocritical against the background of personal creative indulgence.

An example of a church built at the instigation of a patron powerful and rich enough to bear the cost himself was the small one at Shobden in England (*Ill.* 43). The date is again about

1140, at the time of the civil wars of Stephen and Matilda. Its origin is recorded in a contemporary manuscript and has been recounted by Professor Zarnecki as follows: 'It [Shobden Church] was founded by Oliver de Merlimonde, Chief Steward of Hugh de Mortimer, Lord of Wigmore. When the building was begun . . . Oliver went on a pilgrimage to Santiago da Compostella in Spain to pay homage to the relics of St James.' He made the journey by way of France and on his way back he was the guest of the Canons of St Victor in Paris. When the church was finished it was dedicated by Robert de Bethune, Bishop of Hereford. The Abbot of St Victor was then asked to send some of his Canons to Shobden. Here we have all the elements that produced such not entirely monastic foundations. Shobden depended from a powerful and rich man, one who was much preoccupied with religion, since he left his fighting and set out on a pilgrimage. On these travels he consulted religious dignitaries. This is a simple account of a quite modest church—though fairly important for English Romanesque sculpture—and it provides a telling illustration of the individual piety and element of internationalism in the foundation of these churches.

THE TWELFTH-CENTURY PUBLIC

It would be extremely interesting to know just what the sculptures meant aesthetically to the people of the twelfth century, and how they viewed the subject matter. Priestly patrons such as those who commissioned Moissac, Vézelay, Autun or the Cluny capitals obviously fully appreciated their aesthetic quality, but how far it meant anything to anyone outside this small, élite group is very much open to question. It seems most likely that the medieval public, like the Victorians, were either uninterested or more interested in subject matter than in artistic style. Even Abbot Suger gives no real enlightenment, though he does occasionally exhort beholders to marvel not at the

44

richness of the gold and jewels but at the 'workmanship'. It would be interesting to know exactly what Suger meant by this term. There are indications that he may have been concerned, again like the nineteenth century, with technical ingenuity rather than with the overall aesthetic quality and artistic conception, which is what interests most of us today. It is true that Suger continually speaks of such aspects as the beauty of the individual jewels: their quality, colour and translucence, and that he was deeply moved by the effect that all his objects together produced in the church, but he nowhere gives an aesthetic evaluation of the individual works of art as such. It is significant that he does not comment on the sculptures on the outside of his church of St Denis, though he himself must have had them placed there. Perhaps this is a reflection of the reactions of the ordinary man. The emphasis was on homage to God and the inspiration to religious contemplation, and it was for this that the sculptures were valued by all but a minority.

Whatever the reactions of the people of the time to the sculptures may have been, there seems to be absolutely no justification for the assumption, which was made by serious critics as late as the nineteen-thirties, that stylistic peculiarities such as the elongation of figures, or the curious drapery at Autun arose because these people knew no better and were not skilled enough to carve in any other way. This is manifestly absurd for a number of reasons, not least among them the existence of a variety of concurrent styles to which attention has already been drawn. Had the sculptors of 1100 wanted realism there were quite enough classical originals for them to copy—as indeed these were copied a century later. It may be assumed, therefore, that they worked as they did from choice. A like aesthetic preference was expressed by the writer of a recent guide to Autun, who states firmly that: *'Tout compte fait, nous preferons la Vièrge de Giselbert à celle de Raphael.'* Similarly, one might hazard, would those who commissioned the carvings of the early twelfth century. But here we should emphasize 'those who commissioned', the erudite, civilized group, who may have thought purely in their own terms. Soon, in the second half of the century, as the sculptures developed to cover the vast façades of the cathedrals, a new element of public presentation began to creep in and the styles showed a marked change towards a more naturalistic presentation. Besides being effective as part of the new, soaring architecture, these sculptures would also be more easily recognized by the masses in the commercial centres, who were to be instructed by them in the new religious terms.

As the new carvings were to become an integral part of the architectural whole they had, perforce, to be of stone. Stone is heavy and medieval transport facilities were limited, so that the carvings were generally of local stone, the particular qualities of which may well have influenced the work. In addition it was more convenient to bring the sculptors to the site, rather than to allow them to work in their homes or workshops and export the finished wares, as the monastic ivory carvers had done for centuries. And again, while the earlier and smaller churches seem to have been built fairly quickly, the cathedrals, for economic rather than technical reasons, usually took decades or even centuries to build, or were never completed at all. All this ensured that the medieval sculptor would spend a considerable part of his time attached to one or other of these special workshops, and that the individual artist adapted his style to an overall pattern dictated by the master craftsman. The comparative freedom of the monastic workshop was to be replaced by something like regimentation in the cathedral building of the thirteenth century.

Early Gothic

The exact point at which Romanesque moves into Gothic could reasonably be asked if these terms were capable of precise definition. As was stressed in the introductory chapter, this is not so; indeed the confusion is such that for some people the first doors at Chartres (*c*. 1140-50) or the front at Lincoln represent the opening of the Gothic, while for others they are the final flowering of the Romanesque. Neither group is wrong, since each style contains elements of the other, especially as they move into transition. The terms must remain to a large degree subjective, for how can anyone define what is often only an atmosphere, an intellectual or emotional approach? As long as this is accepted and the object is admired, the label is perhaps of only slight importance. But if some criteria must be offered, here most of the transitional mid-century pieces have been assessed as being more influenced by the emotions than by the intellect, and as such have been given the label Gothic rather than Romanesque, for what it is worth. One fact is certain, a dating around 1140 or 1150 is irrelevant to the question. There are many works dating from well into the second half of the century, besides minor carving by what might be regarded as outmoded craftsmen, which are predominantly Romanesque in style, even though they appeared at a time when Gothic was in full flower in the Ile de France. The manuscript-like pair of prophets from Charlieu (*Ill*. 44) may be an example.

The sculpture described as Early Gothic and High Gothic is the visual expression of the triumph of the movement to spiritual reform which began in the eleventh century but only became reasonably effective in the following century. This movement began and flourished in the territories of the King of France (which did not at that time include all the country presently known as France, of which England at times ruled half), and reached its height in the reign of that most ideal and Gothic of all kings, St Louis. It is ironic that the sculptures of the late twelfth and thirteenth centuries, for which more stone was quarried and carved than at any previous time in the world's history, including the whole of Egyptian sculpture, should have been directed to spreading the doctrines of a group of iconoclasts. Yet without the temporal and spiritual advances of the Church the vast sculptural movement of Gothic times would have been impossible.

By the later twelfth century the Church's hold was probably stronger and more far-reaching than at any other period, and one effect of this was the tendency for the authorities everywhere to collaborate in the expansion of the Faith. At home there would be a vast building programme, while abroad lives and treasure continued to be lavished on the Crusades. But the Church's hold depended chiefly on its power to penetrate the daily life of every single individual in an extremely superstitious age.

Sculpture was now more than ever the servant of the Church, publishing the doctrines of this politico-religious organization, the Bible story and its moral and spiritual message, in every new cathedral and parish church throughout the Christian world. This inevitably affected the sculpture's style and content. Gone are the hieratic, mystical statements of the Romanesque, and in their place come figures which, though they may depict saints and worthies, present them as recognizably human with everyday features. They were called upon to illustrate the accepted virtues and vices in a readily understandable way. At the same time they included a little temporal lesson in the kings who represented government, law and order and reminded the passer-by of the feudal system and his position in it.

44 Two Prophets. A capital from Charlieu Abbey, France. Stone, second half of the twelfth century. The heads are badly weathered.

As in the earlier period the sculptures were still mainly concentrated on the porches and tympani or the facades, with lesser works on the corbels and elsewhere. But now the porches and façades of cathedrals become enlarged almost beyond belief. The cathedrals themselves are no longer built for the retreat of an intellectual minority, and hidden away in the comparative obscurity of a monastic complex, but are placed at the centre of the commercial movement and enterprise of a considerable area. They served as a focus and were regarded as an integral part of the developing towns, built for the people and by the people. However cultivated and select the authority directing the programme of sculpture may still have been, it was now the popular didactic approach intended to influence the minds of every man, woman and child that dictated the form and content of the new works. No wonder,

45 Old Testament figures from the West Porch of Chartres Cathedral, France. Stone, mid twelfth century.

then, that the style became far more naturalistic, and the subjects symbolic of practical virtues rather than of philosophical speculations. The biblical or saintly characters were intended as examples to be followed.

In contrast to the opening period of Romanesque, a single sculptural style becomes almost universal. This was no doubt due in part to the scale of the major undertakings, which had to be guided by highly experienced persons normally drawn from one of the established cathedral centres. These artists took with them their pattern books and often their workmen, as well as their own thoughts and ways, and so carried the common style throughout the Western world. While we find some local variations and the influence of certain outstanding masters, most of the carvings of the thirteenth century which are created around the same period are far more closely similar than before. Such changes as there are in the Gothic period

46 (*left*) Christ Blessing, from the South Porch of Chartres Cathedral, France. Stone, early thirteenth century.

47 (*right*) St John, from St Mary's Abbey, York, England. Stone, early thirteenth century.

48 Coronation of the Virgin, the East Tympanum, South Porch of Strasbourg Cathedral, France. Stone, thirteenth century.

49 Procession of Canons. South Porch, Amiens Cathedral, France. Stone, mid thirteenth century.

tend to be the normal stylistic modifications to be expected over a generation rather than the reflections of a series of individual artistic personalities.

We can best appreciate the distinguishing features of the Gothic style, like any other, from observation of examples. The salient feature we find is the development from the late Romanesque linear style to freedom and naturalism by the middle of the thirteenth century.

Around 1150, as at Chartres (*Ill.* 45) or Bourges, the formal stylization is still maintained, with a straight, linear handling of the drapery, by which the already narrow, elongated figures were heightened to appear almost as additional columns to the porches. Yet here the heads begin to lose the hieratic, staring quality and become more naturalistic, and the hands too perform a less stylized role. Nevertheless it would be foolish to claim that the figures, noble though they often are, stand as other than formal symbols. If they express any emotions these are generic rather than personal.

50 The Visitation. Central Porch, Rheims Cathedral, France. Stone, mid thirteenth century.

51 The Signs of the Zodiac and Labours of the Months. West Front, Amiens Cathedral, France. Stone, mid thirteenth century.

In the narrative reliefs too there is a greater naturalism, but they retain something of the Romanesque lively gaiety of spirit even in the Dooms scenes.

By the turn of the century there is a further relaxation of style. The folds become markedly less linear and begin to take on more natural lines. As in the lovely figure of St John from St Mary's Abbey, York (*Ill.* 47), or those on the south porch of Chartres (*Ill.* 46), the faces fill out and the features become much more natural and human. In additon, the statues appear rather more as works of art in their own right and less as architectural adjuncts.

54

From the middle of the thirteenth century these developments culminated in the great and noble sculptures generally regarded as true Gothic. Though still owing its origins to France and often to French or French-trained masters, Gothic had become common to the whole of Europe—at Amiens (*Ill.* 49), Paris, Strasbourg (*Ill.* 48), Westminster, Freiburg or a host of other centres the figures in their flowing nobility presented the ideals of the time, of which we shall say more later. The style was undoubtedly influenced by the conscious adoption of classical models—perhaps the clearest example of this is at Rheims (*Ill.* 50); but for all the naturalism the whole movement is dominated by a sense of dignity and idealization, which seems to arise rather from the search for an almost unattainable nobility of character

52 The Virgin and Child. French, painted oak, thirteenth century. Height 31 in.

53 Foliage capitals from the Chapter House, Southwell Minster, England. Stone, thirteenth century.

presented by the ideal model, than from technical, artistic stylization. It is the spiritual content which marks the Gothic period, quite as much as the aesthetic presentation.

The developments which took place in the figure sculptures are to be found in the reliefs too, though these, curiously enough, show a much more consciously aesthetic handling, as in the decorative arrangement of narrative scenes, or of decorative reliefs like the signs of the zodiac within 'gothic' frames at Amiens (*Ill.* 51).

Of great importance in the history of sculpture at this time are the smaller, more intimate icons of wood or stone that were placed on the altars, or against the pillars within or without the church to attract worshippers. These came to occupy the place hitherto reserved for sacred relics as the focal points of church and pilgrimage. And as the thirteenth century progressed the cult of the Madonna and saints grew, and with it the numbers of figures of the Virgin and Child. In the fourteenth century the same trend continued, and by the fifteenth and early sixteenth centuries there was an enormous production of such objects. At first the majority of icons cling to the hieratic, Romanesque tradition (*Ill.* 52), but they soon develop their own identity. It is not until the later periods that small-scale personal icons develop to any extent.

56

54 Centaur fighting a Dragon, stone roof boss in Westminster Abbey, London. Mid thirteenth century.

Capitals, so important a feature of early Romanesque, still continued, but with the new soaring architecture their sculpture becomes unimportant—generally simple moulding or foliage (*Ill. 53*). It is the bosses and the corbels that become the chief site for decorative carving, and in these the new, simple, naturalistic treatment replaces the more decorative stylizations of earlier artists. Though there may still be some stylization akin to that of the gaming pieces, as in this superb example from Westminster Abbey (*Ill. 54*), the whole composition is more freely conceived.

55 Draughtspiece of walrus ivory, possibly English, dating from the twelfth century. Diameter 2⅞ in.

The sepulchral monument now becomes important, but we shall be considering this development separately.

Curiously enough, ivory carving seems to have declined in the thirteenth century, and apart from the gaming pieces, often of great refinement (*Ill. 55*), lay sculpture remained undeveloped.

If the thirteenth-century figures seem almost too noble to have lived, and so to lack the personal human quality the Renaissance artists were later to create, this is a reflection of the ideals if not always the practices of the times.

The thirteenth century in the North was a period of the highest, almost puritan morality, and the essence of High Gothic is perhaps nowhere better illustrated than in the ideals of the chivalric orders. Richard Coeur de Lion and St Louis have come down to us as the model of Christian warriors, but they stand as the representatives of thousands of idealistic or ambitious men for whom the Crusades presented a wonderful outlet. How many sought fulfilment in this way is shown by the enormous spread of the great militant orders of knighthood. It has been assessed that hundreds of thousands of knights were attached to these orders, and in the succeeding centuries their development as a class was to have wide social repercussions, especially when they had no crusades to occupy them.

The influence of the chivalric ideals on sculpture was seen not only on tombs, which begin to proliferate throughout the land, but also in the ideal of the manly—or for that matter womanly—type to be presented in the sculptures. Nowhere was this better expressed than in the incredible range of the founders' figures at Naumburg, dating from about 1250, nobly represented by Eckehart and Uta (*Ill. 56*).

Also extremely significant in the Naumburg series is the deliberate portrayal of personality, and although this group still retains much of the Gothic dispassion, the idea of presenting psychological types with naked realism is a step towards re-

56 (*left*) Eckehart and Uta. Naumburg Cathedral, Germany. Stone, mid thirteenth century.

57 (*right*) Timo von Kistritz. Naumburg Cathedral, Germany. Stone, mid thirteenth century.

presenting people as individuals with personal characteristics. Particularly remarkable is the presentation of good and evil, the good man and the bad man; a comparison of the figures of Eckehart and Uta with that of Timo von Kistritz (*Ill.* 57) makes the point.

For the medieval man and especially for the sculptors, the issue of the conflict between good and evil was posed on every side. '*Fas et Nefas ambulant paene passu pari*' sang the medieval poet, and what he set in words the sculptors set in stone.

58 The 'Bamberg Rider' from Bamberg Cathedral, Germany. Stone, mid thirteenth century.

Mid Gothic

In his brilliant analysis of the difference between Early and Mid Gothic, Henry Osborne Taylor quotes (in his *The Medieval Mind*) from two chronicles, the first that of de Joinville, the second that of Froissart. The difference between the approaches of these two chronicles is also the difference in the periods, which we see reflected again in the sculptures. In the narrative of de Joinville the old aristocratic knight expresses the punctiliousness of the feudal way of life. This, perhaps, is the keynote of the seriousness reflected in such statues as those at Naumburg or the Bamberg rider (*Ill.* 58). Things may go well or ill for individuals, but nothing must disturb a society ordained by God and devoted to his service. A century later, Froissart's chronicle of a nation is often a tale of knightly individuals fighting their battles for their own honour or in the service of noble ladies.

This change of outlook is so important for sculpture in the late thirteenth and fourteenth centuries that it is worth tracing its origin in more detail. The notion of focusing life round an idealized woman developed into a fairly limited cult as early as the middle of the twelfth century. It was notably expressed, and may indeed have crystallized at the court of the English Queen Eleanor of Aquitaine after her estrangement from King Henry II, when she established herself in her French territories to the south. Here, in company with her daughter Marie, Countess of Champagne, she set up a woman's court of elaborate etiquette and refinement. Amy Kelly describes the situation in her biography of Eleanor: 'The heirs of Poitou and Aquitaine who came to the Queen's high place for their vassal's homage, their squire's training, and their courtier's service, were truculent youths, boisterous young men from the baronial strongholds of the South . . . with little solidarity and no business but local warfare and daredevil escapades . . . These wild young men were a deep anxiety not only to the heads of their houses, but to the Kings of France and England and the Pope in Rome. They were of the stuff of which rebellion and schism are made. For two generations the Church had done what it could with the problem of their unemployment, marching hordes out of Europe on crusades and rounding-up other hordes into the cloister.'

The Queen, ably seconded by her daughter, set out to civilize this rabble, and how successful she was is shown by a contemporary chronicle. 'Time was', the chronicler says, 'when the Bishop of Limoges and the Viscount of Cambourne were content to go in sheep- and fox-skins, but today the humblest would blush to be seen in such poor things. Now they have clothes fashioned of rich and precious stuffs in colours to suit their humour. They snip out the stuff in rings and long slashes to show the lining through, so that they looked like the devils we see in paintings, they slashed their mantles, and their sleeves flow like those of hermits. Youths affect long hair and shoes with pointed toes.'

To promote this advance—or perhaps decadence—a code of chivalry was drawn up by the court chaplain, worked up out of such material as tradition, the *ars amatoria*, or legends like those of King Arthur or Alexander might offer. The basis was militantly feminist and every woman was led to regard her lover as in the same state of vassalage as the Queen's courtiers. As a pastime, the women established a Court of Love before which these courtier knights submitted real or imaginary problems of love. They were sometimes trivial, but they counted sufficiently, nevertheless, to enter and change literature, and condition the whole approach of upper class life. No doubt it was the political success of this experiment as much as its social delights which led the blossoming monarchies of the fourteenth and early fifteenth centuries to adopt it on a much wider scale.

The 'motley bands' recruited into Eleanor's court were not peculiar to Aquitaine nor limited to the twelfth century. They existed throughout Europe, and once the Crusades were over the problem of these people became acute. But now in the third and fourth generation it was aggravated by the very knightliness of the chivalric orders to which they belonged and which had been created for them. They had come to set themselves apart as a privileged class, though frequently without any territorial justification or functions. Whole generations of men had been nurtured on the ideal of military prowess, but were very often without the means to exercise it or to maintain the exclusive life they enjoyed. Consequently they found themselves in the position of Eleanor's young men: a semi-parasitic retainer group, with no outlet but the Church or association with the courts, and dependent on the kings and the great nobles. The pride they affected prevented them from joining the new money-making burgher class.

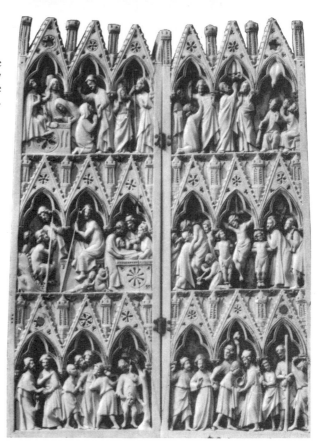

59 Scenes from the Passion. The 'Soissons Diptych'. Ivory, partly coloured and gilded. French, late thirteenth century. Height 12¾ in.

60 The Attack on the Castle of Love. Ivory mirror-case, French or possibly German, mid fourteenth century. Diameter 5⅛ in.

Centuries later Don Quixote is the representative of the best of the chivalric tradition, even if a caricature of elements that were certainly not totally extinguished by the sixteenth century—nor even by the twentieth. Opportunities to pursue their only legitimate profession of war came to them but rarely, so that for most of the time these people had nothing with which to occupy themselves but to play at being knights within the protecting ambit of their feudal overlord. It was for this privileged group the courtois arts evolved. The essential effect of this courtois movement on style in sculpture will immediately be apparent in the illustration opposite. The austerity, idealism and detachment of the Early Gothic gave place to a fashionable court art of models with affected poses of hands and body and smirking faces.

This is especially clear in the small-scale French ivory work, which became so popular both for religious purposes as in the Soissons diptych (*Ill.* 59) and for the caskets or mirror valves,

61 (*far left*) The Virgin and Child. Ivory, French, early fourteenth century. Height 14 in.

62 (*left*) The Deposition. Ivory, French, late thirteenth to fourteenth century. Height 11½ in.

63 (*right*) Madonna of the Rosebush. Painted stone, German, early fourteenth century. Two-thirds life-size.

now frankly for lay interest, illustrating the popular Romances. On such ivory carvings courtois stories and legends found their place. A mirror back (*Ill.* 60) shows a scene in the highest tradition in which a group of knights lay siege to the Castle of Love which is defended by ladies who bombard them with flowers. A charming object, but a silly enough conceit.

This approach changed the faces and figures of sculpture completely: the nobility of Uta is replaced by the smirking of the court lady, whether as model for the Virgin (*Ill.* 63), or for the Christian story generally. From the later part of the thirteenth century and overwhelmingly in the fourteenth, the courtois principles were adopted everywhere. Sculpturally, the treatment is the same whether on trinkets or on church carvings.

It is necessary at this point to turn back a little and touch upon a development which had begun gradually in the thirteenth century and was to have the greatest influence on sculpture as a whole. The rising personal and family cults of the late Middle Ages, whether of the crusading knight or the ruling monarch, led individuals to wish to perpetuate themselves or—even more important in the medieval context—their families and position in the ruling hierarchy. This last the heirs could share. The idea of creating tombs for royal or specially revered persons had always existed, though the practice was fairly restricted and the concern with sculpture very limited. Sometimes there would be simple carvings, such as arms or a crozier, or more rarely a figure, but these tombs were for the most part architectural and followed the form of relic shrines, which in effect they were.

At the beginning of the new development the lead was, of course, given by the tombs of kings or the greater princes, lay or ecclesiastical. These might set the key for a whole sculptural style, but if the royal monuments (*Ill.* 64) offered important commissions for the leading artists, they were naturally exceptional. Fortunately for sculpture, or for the sculptors, the idea percolated rapidly downwards, so that even the modest knightly family felt it incumbent upon it to perpetuate the significance of its ancestry and line by monuments in the village church. The tomb had become a family status symbol. To cater for this

64 Effigy of Henry III in Westminster Abbey, London. Bronze, end of the thirteenth century.

65 (*left*) Head from the effigy of Richard II. Bronze, end of the fourteenth
century.
66 (*right*) Head from the effigy of Edward III. Bronze, late fourteenth
century.

demand workshops grew up—usually at the larger centres—
to which those of any pretension would address themselves.
Though the popularity of these lesser tombs was widespread, it
was not at first sufficiently so to allow for the creation of an
industry on the huge scale that developed in later centuries, when
everyone had a tombstone.

At the outset there seems to have been little or no attempt
at portraiture or exact personal representation even on the royal
monuments, and it is not until we come to the middle of the
fourteenth century or a little later, with examples such as the
tombs of Richard II and Edward III in Westminster Abbey

67 Horseman from the tomb of Aymer de Valance, Earl of Pembroke. Westminster Abbey, London. Painted stone, early fourteenth century.

(*Ills.* 65, 66), that portraiture becomes more important—though even then it was rare. In the early stages, especially for the tombs of the less elevated (*Ill.* 12) a stock figure sufficed. Throughout Europe there are endless numbers of similar crusader knights lying on their monuments, sometimes accompanied by their ladies in contemporary costume. Individuality is provided by the inscriptions, and above all by the coats-of-arms. Although the tombs are seldom of outstanding artistic merit, they nevertheless had the virtue of offering employment and a school for young sculptors as cathedral building waned.

If the first important monuments had been fairly simple, by the later thirteenth century, and increasingly during the fourteenth, ancillary sculptural devices, such as the horsemen on the tomb of Aymer de Valance of 1325 (*Ill.* 67) or angels supporting the head of the deceased came to play a prominent part. Ultimately, in later examples such as the tombs of the Dukes of Burgundy at Dijon (*Ill.* 68), major artists created important works of sculpture in which the tomb element is almost secondary—at least for us today. So the way was paved for the development of the secular monument, which, as church carvings declined, became the principle outlet for sculpture right through to the twentieth century.

68 Tomb of Jean sans Peur. Painted alabaster, Franco-Flemish, *c.* 1400.

Late Gothic

So far we have traced some of the influences which have changed styles in sculpture from the twelfth to the end of the fourteenth century. With the fifteenth century a whole fresh chain of events and change in society produced yet another stylistic revolution. If the Romanesque or Early Gothic carvings were influenced almost entirely by the ideas of the Church, and those of the fourteenth century reflected the court graces, those of the fifteenth century represent the new social order of the nation, headed by the king and supported largely by the wealth of the great cities, which meant the new burgher classes. Religious themes may still have predominated, but a new twist was give by the century's political, economic and social developments.

If any had profited and advanced in a century of economic and military disaster, it was the townsfolk and the burgesses, who pursued such trade as they could and used the advantages that their money gave them to gain concessions from the hard-pressed kings and potentates. Their rise had begun in earlier centuries, but throughout this period they had striven to consolidate their position within the feudal hierarchy, usually in association with the Crown and at the expense of the warring privileged classes. Fifteenth-century sculpture reflects their success among the other elements of the time. The models were no longer mainly idealized leaders or noble persons standing for saints and virtues, but a much more middle-class group of ordinary people, naturalistically presented. The Gothic impersonality remains, nevertheless; the sculptured figures were not to appear fully individualized until after the Renaissance. A comparison of illustrations 69 and 84 makes this point. In the single figures or multiple narrative groups of the new altarpieces or screens straight representationalism prevails, and the sacred story is conveyed by models who were knights or burghers, peasants or aldermen, and recognizable as such, as they would be in the mystery plays. If kings still featured occasionally, as at Canterbury, this emphasized the political aspect of monarchy.

In order to account for the decline—at least for the decline in quantity—of sculpture by the later fourteenth century, and this complete change in style in the renewed activity in the fifteenth, we are forced to turn to the traditional reasons—the war, economic disasters and the plagues that brought ruin everywhere. The Hundred Years' War—which had started in the 1300s and was perhaps only an intensification of traditional feudal struggles—ensured that in France and England, at any rate, what plague left of the economy was given almost entirely to war. It was guns before butter, and certainly before sculpture—literally so, indeed, if we are to believe the classic story that the sculptors of Rheims were employed to carve stone cannon balls for the newly invented guns. The wars and disasters could only harm the arts, for even when there was a little money to be spared the factions were far too occupied in building and rebuilding undecorated castles to interest themselves in elaborately sculptured churches, of which there was a sufficiency in any event. For these various reasons the demand for the latter fell off, and with its falling off, the whole outlook of sculpture changed. The minds of the pious turned from church building and sculptured façades towards decorating the existing interiors with figures of saints, altarpieces, stalls and misericords, which now became the main outlet for religious sculpture.

The new objects were on a far smaller scale than the façade sculpture, and this meant that private buyers or groups of modest means could afford to commission works. This in turn changed the technical and production needs, and the materials. The large groups of artists who had hitherto been attached to some vast

69 St Catherine in Prison. Painted alabaster, English, fifteenth century.
Height 16⅜ in.

building operation were able to split up and establish local workshops. Instead of travelling to work on the site, they could carve
at home and export their wares to the churches or patrons who
needed them. Such smaller workshops with local ties tended

72

70 Altarpiece from Oplinter. Antwerp, oak, late fifteenth century.

to develop an individuality in their products as against the comparative homogeneity of the great cathedral sculptures.

Organized under various guilds, the carvers developed what was virtually a wholesale business and mass production of sculpture, reaching enormous proportions by the end of the fifteenth century.

Most important of all, the war-torn Ile de France was no longer the dominating inspirational centre, but rather the prosperous towns of Flanders and Southern Germany, and the carvings take on a new character from the change.

An example of this new type of production for export is to be found in the alabaster workshops of England (*Ill.* 69) which delivered their wares abroad as well as at home. Even more highly organized, and producing work of greater aesthetic merit, were the great sculptors' guilds of Flanders and the North at the end of the century, such as those of Brussels, Malines, Antwerp (*Ill.* 70) or Lübeck, all with ready access to the sea and cheap transport. Most of these supplied objects of all sizes, from small devotional figures intended for the private home to vast altarpieces many feet high, showing elaborate Crucifixion groups crowded with figures, or scenes from the lives of the saints.

These large works were all carried out in easily-transportable sections perhaps 18 inches to 2 feet long, which were assembled on the site to create the larger complex. The majority of Flemish and German carvings in museums and private collections today originally belonged to such altarpieces. At Brussels and Antwerp the business was so highly organized that Guild stamps were applied to each separate unit so that there could be no doubt as to their origin. They were marked as though they were pieces of plate.

Encouraged by the new civic pride, similar centres developed in the leading southern towns too, notably at Ulm, Nuremberg and Augsburg, although there the markets seem to have been more local.

For all this type of work, since the sculptures had to be transported and no longer needed to withstand the weather, wood came increasingly to take the place of stone. Besides being easier to transport, it was easier to carve, and covered with a layer of gesso it could be painted with the lively, vigorous colours and gilding that were favoured by current decorative taste.

The qualities of the various local woods had an undoubted influence on the stylistic variations which developed during this period. We can see, for instance, how the styles of the oak carvings of the north, with their rather sharp, broad cut planes were dictated by the hardness of the material, while the comparative ease with which limewood could be carved into almost

71 The Flagellation, from a painted and gilded stone altarpiece. French, first half of the sixteenth century. Height of detail, about 30 in.

any sort of fantastic contortion without splitting or breaking, permitted full play to the fantasies which were to spring from the late Gothic mind in the Rhineland and southern Germany.

In certain areas where suitable stone was easier to come by, such as northern and eastern France with its fine chalkstone, it still remained popular as a material, though unless reduced to the scale of the alabaster carvings in England it was always more difficult to transport, so that we find no export development of stone carvings comparable to that of the wood carving of Flanders or even southern Germany.

Still another factor of considerable importance to sculpture was the change that took place during this later period in the attitude of the individual towards the devotional figures. A new, intimate, almost anthropomorphic approach was adopted towards the statuettes of the Virgin and Child or the popular saints, or the representations of one or other of the many cults which began to proliferate all over the Catholic world. The carvings were endowed by the worshippers with supernatural powers, if not with living characteristics; and now, rather than to the sacred relics, it was to the figure in the corner of the room or to the saint against the pillar or to the altarpiece that the individual addressed his personal intercession. This new attitude must have had much to do with the increasing humanity of the carvings. Whether this religious development, which included so much that was virtually idolatry, arose because the figures were already there, or whether instead the sculptures merely increased in number to meet the religious demand is a question which we should not immediately attempt to answer. But facts and commonsense both indicate that the two developments were mutually encouraging. In any event, by the sixteenth century the religious movement had become so intense that it provided a major platform for the reformers, and was held to justify their disastrous iconoclasm, with its ruinous effects on sculpture as a whole.

72 Claus Sluter: Angel from the *Puits de Moïse* (Well of Moses), Dijon, France. Stone, *c.* 1400.

73 Madonna and Child. Painted stone, French, mid fifteenth century. Half life-size.

Each of the factors we have outlined, or all of them taken together, might suggest that the art of the period would move towards a hard-headed realism, and this in fact is just what happened.

Even by the late fourteenth century, the courtois affectations of smile and gesture have become modified and the figures no longer 'sway' as in the ivory Madonna (*Ill.* 61). The drapery is still simple, but now falls into more natural, less posed folds. This was the trend over the whole of the north of Europe.

A last flowering of the chivalrous, courtly, romantic tradition took place at the end of the fourteenth and start of the fifteenth century, in the regions comparatively free from the major conflict: in Burgundy, and also in the southern German territories of the Empire, even as far away as Bohemia. The Sluter figures of the *Puits de Moïse* (*Ill.* 72), and, of course, those on the outstanding tombs of the Dukes at Dijon illustrate the French variant of the style. They all date from the first years of the fifteenth century. The spirit is still maintained in the slightly later, exquisite and lyrical Madonna from Toulouse (*Ill.* 73).

74 *Pietà*. Painted and gilded wood. South German, early fifteenth century. Height 30 in.

75 (*left*) Madonna and Child. Painted and gilded wood, German, fifteenth century.

76 (*right*) St Peter, the West façade of Regensburg Cathedral, Germany. Stone, early fifteenth century.

Partly reflecting the same spirit but for the rest springing from separate sources was the charming series of figures, not always Madonnas, but often known as the school of the '*Schoënen Madonnen*' (*Ill.* 74). This style, which spread across South Germany in particular, carried on the grace and prettiness of the fourteenth century—slightly humanized and perhaps slightly *déclassé*, but nevertheless of the greatest lyrical charm. A typical expression is seen in the elaborate play of the folds of drapery

77 Hans Multscher: St George and St John the Evangelist, Ulm Cathedral, Germany. Stone, mid fifteenth century.

78 (*left*) Michael Pacher: Head of St Michael. Painted wood, German, late fifteenth century.

79 (*right*) Figure of a Saint from the Cathedral at Hal, Belgium. Stone, fifteenth century.

of the Regensburg St Peter (*Ill.* 76). But soon, by the middle decades of the fifteenth century, the trend towards representational naturalism was everywhere apparent. It is superbly illustrated by the example from Hans Multscher of Ulm (*Ill.* 77), where the whole rendering reaches a stage of unaffected simplicity at times almost photographic.

This naturalistic approach was to reach its highest development in the workshops of Flanders, whose influence became increasingly important as the fifteenth century went on. With the export of both objects and artists the Low Countries rapidly came to play a dominant part in North European sculpture—one that was to continue for a long time to come—not only in the immediately neighbouring areas of Northern France and Germany, but in

England and Spain, too. The fashion for realistic detail which was so marked in the Flemish paintings is reflected in the carvings. Whether in larger-scale works such as the figures from Hal (*Ill.* 79) or in the mass-produced saints and altarpieces, the factual nature of the representation outweighs all other features. The folds are natural, the eyes and features clearly cut. Details of ornament such as jewellery, daggers, belts or armour are clearly drawn. In all this there is often curiously little concession to general aesthetic effect, or indeed to any apparent ideal of beauty, either in the execution or the choice of models.

This move towards what might be called 'unvarnished truth' was to develop, later in the century and especially in the south, into a new, formal starkness. The harsher aspects of life were highlighted and almost hysterically exaggerated in gruesome martyrdoms and deaths, or in the *Pietàs*, Entombments and Crucifixion details so popular with the new Germanic cults. An early version of this extremism is the superb but horrifying *Pietà* from Bonn (*Ill.* 80). This type of religious and artistic approach

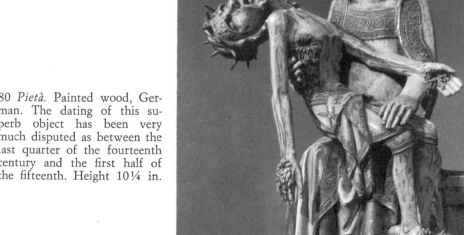

80 *Pietà*. Painted wood, German. The dating of this superb object has been very much disputed as between the last quarter of the fourteenth century and the first half of the fifteenth. Height 10¼ in.

continued to find favour, particularly in Germanic areas, throughout the fifteenth and into the sixteenth century. Though not perhaps so theatrical as the Bonn group, the handling is harsh enough in works such as the great altar by Michael Pacher (*Ill.* 81). The angular figures are set in a housing of ornamental tracery which had no doubt developed from Early Gothic foliage and canopy carving, but is as like to them as a thorn bush to a feather bed.

The style continues in the altarpieces of Veit Stoss, and even in his superb small boxwood Madonna (*Ill.* 82), which reflects

81 (*left*) Michael Pacher: Detail from the St Wolfgang Altar, St Wolfgang, Germany. Painted wood, later fifteenth century.

82 (*right*) Veit Stoss: The Virgin and Child. Boxwood, German, early sixteenth century. Height 8½ in.

83 (*left*) Nicolas Gerhardt: The Virgin and Child with St Anne. Stone, German, third quarter of the fifteenth century. Height 25 in.

84 (*right*) Detail of the Virgin and Child. Painted wood, German, later fifteenth century. Height of whole figure 41½ in. Sometimes ascribed to Simon Lainberger.

the same uncompromisingly rugged, almost brutal qualities in the cutting of the folds and the choice of the model. This last is certainly significant. Here the Virgin is a peasantwoman, or is, at least, certainly no noblewoman, and is very far removed from the spirit that conceived the ivory Virgin of a century and a half earlier. This is a Germanic art of wars and dungeons and tortures rather than of ideals or love. At the same time not all was sadism, and alongside the violence some lyricism still persists. The group of the Holy Family by Nicolas Gerhardt (*Ill.* 83) or the Dangolsheim Madonna in Berlin ascribed to Simon Lainberger (*Ill.* 84) are as lyrical as a della Robbia or a Rossellino. At times this delicacy of feeling falls into sentimentality—a distinction not always sharp in German thought. The tendency seems to

85 Tilman Riemenschneider: Detail of group. Limewood, German, late fifteenth century.

be present in these superb figures by perhaps the greatest carver of the turn of the century, Tilman Riemenschneider (*Ills.* 85, 86). In these later works, while realism dictated the treatment of the heads and hands, the drapery began to take on an increasing artificiality and stylization, folded and pleated in a totally un-

86

86 Tilman Riemenschneider: Salome, from a group of the Holy Kindred.
Limewood, German, early sixteenth century. Half life-size.

natural if decorative manner (*Ill.* 85). Designs were readily passed from one workshop to another by drawings and engravings, and it would seem that these new features in sculpture —which are essentially graphic rather than plastic—were evolved from graphic sources, rather than the other way about.

Outside Flanders and the German territories much the same influence prevailed, but the general quality is seldom so high, and perhaps the naturalism succumbs less to stylistic exaggeration at the end of the century. Little comparable to the Breissach altar (*Ill.* 94) appears elsewhere in the North. English work owed almost everything to Flemish influence and Flemish carvers. Figures such as those of Henry V's Chapel, or for that matter Henry VII's, would occasion no surprise if found in the Low Countries. The same holds true for Spain.

In France the movement towards naturalism persisted throughout the fifteenth century. It is particularly marked in the large Entombment groups, so popular in the North (*Ill.* 87). Yet

87 Mourning over the Dead Christ. Stone, French, sixteenth century.

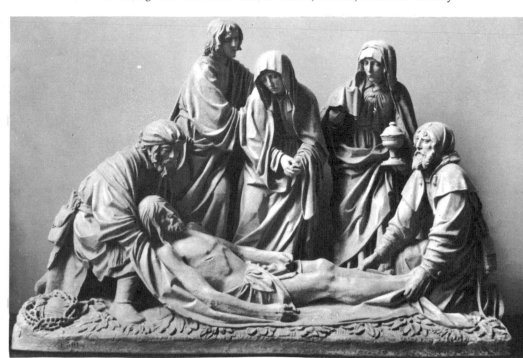

if these are life-like, there is nothing of the marked brutality of works from across the Rhine, and a certain Gallic lyricism pervades even these harsher representations. In the Troyes Madonnas, for instance, an almost Renaissance humanity prevails.

THE EARLY SIXTEENTH CENTURY

We have placed the whole of the splendid group of early sixteenth century Flemish and German works under the heading 'late Gothic', rather than 'Renaissance', because it is a very moot point whether any Northern European sculpture was truly Renaissance in spirit. Just as Gothic was never really understood by the Italians, so the intellectual humanism and open lyrical sensuality of the Florentine Quattrocento were seldom adopted wholeheartedly in the North.

By 1500 some deference was generally paid to the Renaissance vocabulary of ornament, but often in a rather uncomprehending way. Not until the second or even third decades of the century were a classical naturalism in treatment, or a classical-allegorical subject-matter adopted at all widely. Even then, what we have is usually a purely formal adaptation of the appearance of the style rather than an absorption of the underlying ideas. There is a modified form of linear naturalism in the rendering of drapery or the features but little real appreciation of the Renaissance spirit. Even as late as the 1520s, the whole conception of the great Antwerp altars belongs entirely to the earlier generation.

This reserve was no doubt due partly to the Reforming spirit, but also to the essential conservatism of the still-feudal Northern society. And it was reinforced by the attitude of the strongly-established guild organizations, which were by nature hostile to the Renaissance ideal of individual expression and personal artistic independence.

The examples which show some Renaissance sensibility do so chiefly in acceptance of details of ornament, occasionally with more naturalistic representation of the figures. The crowding of the groups and the almost total lack of feeling for flow of line or overall design of the sculptures (as distinct from that of the architectural housing) carries on the schematic treatment of the mass-export altarpieces of the fifteenth century.

In all these works the intention was that the story should strike the beholder, rather than the work of art, just as it had been ever since the Gothic break with Romanesque. Artistic appreciation was increasingly directed towards technical virtuosity and elaboration, introduced for its own sake, to become an exercise in dexterity. The idea that the subject matter could be chiefly a pretext or vehicle, allowing the artist to produce a personal aesthetic interpretation and a work of art seems to have been repugnant to the Northern morality. No doubt the restriction of sculpture in the Protestant countries to sepulchral monuments, or to architectural details in churches or cathedrals —or in the homes to fire-places, overmantels or ornaments—helped to inhibit sculptors from creating objects of great beauty. But the Italian creations of the fifteenth century in these fields suggest that this practical reason was not the main one. And indeed, once the court Mannerist tradition had become well established towards the latter half of the sixteenth century, sculptors did occasionally manage to achieve attractive work in these directions.

This persistent attachment to Gothic forms and traditions is remarkably illustrated in one of the outstanding achievements of Western sculpture—the tombs of Margaret of Austria, her husband Philibert le Beau and her mother Margaret of Bourbon, executed under the direction of Conrad Meit of Worms as late as the 1530s (*Ill.* 88). In his small boxwood carvings or in the alabaster figure at Munich (*Ill.* 91) Meit shows himself as one of the most successful Renaissance-minded Northern carvers of his day. In the tombs at Brou in France, however, both the overall setting and the details of execution are largely Gothic in conception.

We are fortunate that the contracts which show the terms on which these monuments were done are still extant. The general supervision was to be by Conrad Meit, but the extent to which the patrons could expect his personal intervention is shown by the fact it was found necessary to insert a specific clause—even in this royal commission—which insisted that at least the heads and hands of the main figures were to be the work of the master himself. A similar example of Gothic overall design and Renaissance detail is to be found in the great bronze shrine of St Sebald of the Church of the Saint at Nuremberg. Here we find purely Gothic housing, architectural design and figures suddenly combined with small individual sculptures by the Vischer workshop that are truly Renaissance in spirit and of extremely high quality (*Ills.* 89, 90).

88 Conrad Meit: Tomb of Philibert le Beau of Savoy at Brou, France. Alabaster, German, third decade of the sixteenth century.

These examples all emphasize that in the North it was only in a few artists—and then almost entirely in small works—that we find anything approaching a truly Renaissance spirit.

The development of lay *Kleinplastik* was very important, though limited in the main to Germany, with some reflection in Flanders. No doubt it was the widespread manufacture of small personal icons for religious purposes in the fifteenth century that gave rise to the development of lay carvings and small-scale reliefs and figures. At their best these are distinguished from the religious pieces of the earlier period by their intention to please as works

89,90 Peter Vischer: *left*, Hercules, a detail from the Shrine of St Sebald, height 10¼ in.; *right*, the Shrine of St Sebald, Sebaldskirche, Nuremberg. Bronze, second decade of the sixteenth century.

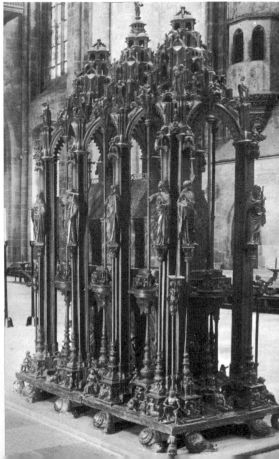

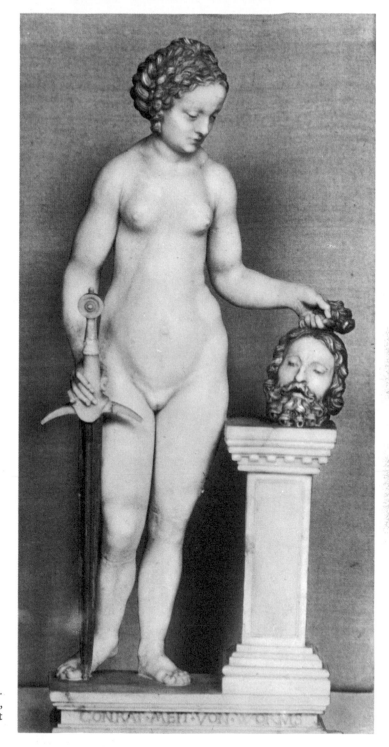

1 Conrad Meit: *Judith*.
Painted Marble, German,
sixteenth century. Height
11¾ in.

92 Portrait of an unknown man. Boxwood, German, sixteenth century. Diameter 2¼ in.

93 (below) A. Daucher: Christ with Mary and St John, Fugger Chapel, Church of St Anne, Augsburg, Germany. Stone, early sixteenth century.

of art, quite apart from any functional or religious purpose. They became increasingly popular, and the greatest artists readily created objects in boxwood or ivory or bronze or precious metals for their rich and princely patrons, just as at the Renaissance in Italy, or, indeed, in classical times. Alongside this type of work there were the portrait medals which had begun to assume great importance in the Italian Renaissance, and were to continue elsewhere most successfully during the next century. They made excellent keepsakes, like the portrait photographs of today, and

94 Master H. L.: Altarpiece from Breisach, Germany. Limewood, second decade of the sixteenth century.

developed into a considerable industry. Heights of craftsmanship were reached by the boxwood examples from Germany (*Ill.* 92), which have never been equalled.

Apart from these, only occasional works, such as the group executed by Adolf Daucher for the Fugger Chapel at Augsburg (*Ill.* 93) show more Renaissance than Gothic characteristics. Even Daucher's other work was mainly Gothic. If there was any change in the North before the Mannerist inventions of the mid-century it was rather in a strange new handling of drapery for decorative ends, as we see in the Breisach altar (*Ill.* 94), which is almost Baroque in its ebullience.

95 Giovanni Pisano: *Haggai*. Executed for the façade of Siena Cathedral, probably in 1285-95. Marble, 24 in. high.

The Trecento

The history of Italian art is the history of the individuals who
created it. In the North the individual and his work is su-
bordinate to the trend of the period, be it Gothic or Rococo,
and dozens of works by different artists may all be equally valid
as illustrations of a single stylistic development. In Italy, on
the other hand, except in the very broadest of terms, the 'trend'
is an entirely artificial structure, imposed by critics for convenience in classification, and artists and their works cannot be
interchanged in the same fashion. Of the North it may be said
quite accurately that 'a movement arose', but in Italy it is always
'the artist X or the artist Y did such and such a thing'. This
situation largely dictates the approach of any general introduction
to Italian sculpture, and here, although certain themes can be
traced for short periods, it is only possible within the limits imposed to lay out a chart of the subject and suggest the more
important relationships between the component parts. Naturally
a ruthless pruning is unavoidable if the overall picture is to retain
any clear shape, and since this is essentially a personal process no
apology is made for the vast range of omissions.

Although the term 'Italian Gothic' is in general use, 'Gothic' in
this context stands as much in need of qualification as does the
term 'Renaissance' when employed in connection with territories
north of the Alps. Group activity and the essential Gothic qualities of detached idealism and impersonality were all basically
unsympathetic to the temperament of at least the Latin areas of
Italy (as opposed to the North Italian area running from Liguria through Lombardy to the Veneto, and Angevin dominated
Southern Italy including Naples and Sicily). Where the Gothic

style did flourish in Italy it did not emerge until more than a hundred years later than in the North, and then pursued a highly individualistic course.

In the hands of the Pisani, or artists like Arnolfo di Cambio and Tino di Camaino and their followers, this Italian Gothic style took on a personal sculptural quality that bears little relationship to the ordered, formal and detached beauty of Northern Gothic. And indeed it is significant that we immediately think of Italian Gothic sculptures as the work of individual artists, rather than as anonymous group or workshop activities associated with a particular town or cathedral.

Despite the unfavourable Latin predisposition, the initial focus of the indigenous Italian Gothic style lay in Tuscany, and, in particular, in the activities of the astounding family of the Pisani, starting with the work of Nicola Pisano in the middle of the thir-

96 Nicola Pisano: Relief of the Crucifixion. Marble, *c.* 34 in. high. The pulpit in Pisa decorated by the relief is signed and dated 1260.

teenth century and continuing with his son Giovanni from *c.*1275 to his death after 1314. The earliest sculpture by Nicola Pisano, that decorating the pulpit in the Baptistery at Pisa, derives its inspiration directly from Roman sarcophagi and other classical sources—not only for the lay-out and composition, but for the whole dynamic drama of the handling (*Ill.* 96). We can, however, follow the transition from this Late Romanesque (or proto-Renaissance) style to the Gothic—under the influence of Nicola's son Giovanni—through the series of great pulpits executed by the family and its studio in Pisa, Siena and Pistoia.

The Gothic style of architecture had first been introduced into Italy by the Cistercians some eighty years earlier in such buildings as the Abbey at Fossanova, but for sculpture the new style spread into Italy through the medium of ivories and small-scale metalwork, along the trade route linking France and the Angevin kingdom of Naples. This route led down the coast from Liguria as far as Pisa, swinging inland to Siena and avoiding Florence before continuing southwards, which goes far to explain the strength of the Gothic style in Pisa and Siena and the shortness of its reign in Florence.

Giovanni Pisano's sculpture decorating the pulpit in Pisa Cathedral shows the impact of the Gothic style in a new wealth of naturalistic observation, and in a certain softness that replaces the rigid formality of Nicola's figures—a change illustrated by the contrast between the massive grave figure of *Fidelity* by Nicola in the Baptistery at Pisa (*Ill.* 97) and the intimate, lyrical figure of a Deacon by Giovanni, which fulfils a parallel role on the later pulpit in S. Andrea at Pistoia (*Ill.* 98), or Giovanni's marble Madonna and Child carved for the Arena Chapel in Padua, where the hieratical qualities of a 'Queen of Heaven bearing the Little Emperor' are replaced by the intimacy of the relationship between an earthly mother and child. But although the emphasis is now on the human characteristics of the figure and its personal relationship with the observer, Giovanni's Madonnas

97 Nicola Pisano: *Fidelity*. Marble, 23 in. high. This allegorical figure carries a dog, his symbol, and is part of the same pulpit in Pisa as *Ill. 96*.

98 (*right*) Giovanni Pisano: A Deacon. Marble, 35 in. high. The pulpit in Pistoia decorated by this figure is dated 1301.

never attempt to emulate the sweetness and frivolity of many of their French models. The same characteristics are to be seen in the great monumental series from the Baptistery at Pisa and his large-scale figure work on the cathedral at Siena (*Ill.* 95). The heavy weathering of this fragment make it difficult for us to be certain of the original surface handling, but the illustration reveals the planning, and emphasizes that the relationship between the architecture and the carved figure in Italy was totally different from that in the North (cf. *Ills.* 95, 46, 47).

Apart from works like these and a few fountains such as the Fontana Maggiore at Perugia (*Ill.* 101), the main outlet for the sculptor in Italy in Gothic times was the personal monument in the church. It would seem that in the Italian peninsula, in contrast to the North, the emphasis was on the painted rather than the sculptured icon, so that carved representations of Madonnas and saints are relatively few. Extremely elaborate monuments, on the other hand, are to be found at most centres throughout Italy. For the most part the concentration is on the architectural whole rather than on the individual sculptures, which are not always of very high quality. They consist of a recumbent figure lying on a tomb chest, which may be variously carved with scenes, arms, saints, or busts in panels, all set under a tall baldacchino following the principles of a shrine. Among

99 (*left*) Tino di Camaino: Monument of Mary of Valois, S. Chiara, Naples. Marble, *c*. 1331-3. Damaged 1940-45.

100 (*right*) Nino Pisano: Angel of the Annunciation. Pigmented wood, approximately life-size. The figure probably dates from *c*. 1350-68.

101 (*left*) Giovanni Pisano: A Prophet. Marble, 24½ in. high. The fountain in Perugia decorated by this figure was completed in 1278. Nicola Pisano also worked on the fountain, and it is not certain whether this figure represents his latest work or Giovanni's earliest.

102 (*right*) Tino di Camaino: *Charity*. Marble, 39 in. high. Detail of the monument to Catherine of Austria in S. Lorenzo Maggiore, Naples. The work on this monument was recorded as being in progress in 1323.

the most elaborate are those in Verona, and in Naples where Tino di Camaino and his school reached a rather higher quality than was general (*Ill. 99*). In these earlier works the influence of the Pisani is strong, and there are certain broad characteristics that distinguish them from their Northern counterparts. The superb *Charity* by Tino (*Ill. 102*) and the relief from the Annibaldi Monument by Arnolfo (*Ill. 105*) are typical in their overall

103 (*left*) Nino Pisano: *Madonna del Latte*. This marble group probably dates from the 1360s. Height 35 in.

104 (*right*) Lorenzo Maitani: Two Angels from the façade of Orvieto Cathedral. Marble, *c.* 24 in. high, executed between 1310 and 1330.

105 Arnolfo di Cambio: *Frieze of Mourning Acolytes*. Marble with 'cosmati work' background, 28 in. high. A fragment of the monument (now dismembered) to Cardinal Annibaldi della Molara in Rome, 1276. The attribution to Arnolfo is on stylistic grounds. The relief can be compared to Northern versions, such as that on the South Porch at Amiens (see *Ill.* 49).

106 Andrea Orcagna: The Burial of the Virgin. This marble relief is signed and dated 1359. Height *c.* 48 in.

simplification of the draperies, and their particular round jowly type of face with small, rather pig eyes.

During the course of the fourteenth century the French influence strengthens. It is apparent in Giovanni Pisano's marble Madonna from the Arena Chapel mentioned earlier, but above all in the lovely series of figures in stone and wood by Nino Pisano, which might indeed be French were it not for the Italian simplification of the draperies. This is one of the most striking features of his beautiful *Madonna del Latte* (*Ill.* 103), which, despite the linear silhouette that owes so much to painting, is essentially plastic in its simple volumes. The closest approach in the Latin areas to Northern Gothic sculpture is probably provided by Lorenzo Maitani's reliefs decorating the façade of Orvieto Cathedral (*Ill.* 104), and in these the debt to graphic art is even more striking.

The Black Death struck Italy in 1349, followed by an economic crisis that brought about a sharp break in sculptural activity, so that, with the exception of Andrea Orcagna's shrine in Orsanmichele in Florence (*Ill.* 106), the sculptural scene remained extremely barren until the closing decade of the century.

104

The Quattrocento

The concept of the Renaissance has no chronological or geographical significance, and indeed can mean almost anything that an author chooses to make it mean, but for the purposes of this book it can be identified with that rational and scientific conception of the world—Humanism—which has its roots in medieval and classical thought and is the basis of our modern civilization.

Humanism is essentially that philosophical movement at the close of the Middle Ages which asserted the right of the individual to the use of his own reason and to belief in the validity of his conclusions, in opposition to the sterility of late medieval scholasticism. This fresh approach, of allowing the individual to reason out a problem on his own account instead of learnedly searching earlier texts, was in part the result of renewed study of classical texts in their original forms, which in turn encouraged further study of the Classics, so that, once initiated, the movement spread rapidly. Experimental science blossomed forth immediately when men again began to look at natural processes and then analyse their observations instead of merely consulting their Aristotle. A fundamental change in the approach to image-making followed, for although in Gothic naturalism the medieval artist might have been a very acute observer of nature, with the new movement came scientific and analytical naturalism.

The new dignity of the individual finds its parallel in the new figure sculpture, for in the Renaissance a statue's form is no longer merely the symbol for its content, as in Gothic sculpture, but becomes the vehicle by which the content is conveyed. As

Alberti writes in his *De Statua*, it is through the gestures of the body that the mind is expressed. This imbuing of the statue with a clearly-defined personality, reacting in a logical and personal fashion to its environment, opened up whole new ranges of emotional relationships for sculpture. Expression was now no longer confined in the main to the head and hands, but was conveyed by the whole body and with the drapery fulfilling an essential role instead of a largely decorative function.

The Renaissance is essentially an Italian phenomenon and marks the return of Italian art to a style entirely suited to the Italian temperament.

FLORENCE

During the Trecento the conflict between the two rival factions, the Guelph party who supported the Emperor and the Ghibellines who favoured the Pope, had lost its meaning but little of its virulence, and knowledge of the political alignment of the various states and cities of Italy is most important for an understanding of the subsequent course of events. The political centre of gravity of Central Italy shifted from Ghibelline Siena with her traditional political and artistic ties with Gothic France, to Guelph Florence, which had been left independent by the waning influence in Italy of the Holy Roman Emperor and the death of his vassal, Gian Galeazzo Visconti, Duke of Milan, a fact extremely significant for the arts.

Florence recovered only slowly from the economic collapse following the Black Death and the failure of the great banks, and suffered further from prolonged Milanese economic and military pressure, but shortly before 1400 she regained her stability, and from then on took the lead in artistic developments. Indeed, the evolution of Renaissance sculpture may be summarized in the statement that the style emerged in Florence in the first quarter of the Quattrocento and spread during the remaining three-quarters to the remainder of Italy, penetrating to the Gothic

107 Donatello: *Dancing Children*. Marble relief on the external pulpit of the Cathedral, Prato. Executed between 1428 and 1438.

centres of Northern Italy late in the century. Florence occupies the central position in this process and in the first three-quarters of the century almost every leading sculptor was Florentine.

PATRONAGE

During the Trecento, patronage in the Republics of Florence, Siena and Venice had been mainly ecclesiastical in character, in contrast to that of the Gothic princely courts in the valley of the Po, at Naples and in other, smaller towns, where the major commissions were mostly for imposing tombs to commemorate their secular rulers. But during the Quattrocento there began in Florence a complicated interplay of influence between the increasing secularization of art due to the rise of Humanism and the changing character of the patronage.

During the first half of the century great *entrepreneurs*—either as private patrons or as members of the great commercial guilds—provided the backbone of progressive patronage and modified the traditional monopoly of the Church; but in the second half the children and grandchildren of these patrons formed a new privileged class that looked for inspiration in its leisure to the courts, and provided an increasingly conservative element. Another change in the character of patronage is illustrated by Cosimo de' Medici and his grandson Lorenzo, for while the former was essentially a creator, the founder of churches and monasteries, the latter was exclusively a collector. Thus while the robust, realist tradition of Florentine art favoured by the first generation continued throughout the century, Quattrocento art of the second half tends to become increasingly elegant and graceful, approaching more closely the art of the courts, where Renaissance forms, if not always the Renaissance spirit, were growing in influence.

The Quattrocento also witnessed a profound change in the status of the artist. The Humanists loosened the bonds of the craft tradition, recognizing the intellectual status of creative artists and placing them beside writers, musicians and philosophers—a process partly the result of a complete misunderstanding of the classical texts, where the position of classical artists as the intimate friends of rulers was taken to be an intellectual standing. In fact the fine arts had never been classed with the liberal arts, and the artist in classical times always remained an artisan no matter what airs he adopted. The stranglehold of the guild-apprentice system was finally broken, and by the end of the century schools such as that in the 'Giardino Mediceo' gave a less formal training and took over many of the teaching functions of the workshops—to give way in turn in the sixteenth century to the academies.

Thus although the artists were emancipated from their dependence upon the Church and the medieval craft guilds, they had now become even more intimately dependent upon the Humanists; but at least in this position they were no longer regarded as servants, as they had been by the theologians of the Trecento. This close association with the Humanists also produced a shift of attention from the production *per se* to the production as a manifestation of the personality of the master, which arose from the Renaissance conception of the work of art as the creation of a unique genius. This was followed by the recognition of genius as the capacity to achieve, rather than mere recognition of genius in the achievement—an important step which led in turn to an increasing interest in the processes of artistic creation, and to a growing demand for unfinished works and preparatory drawings, prompted by the belief that thereby the beholder reached a closer understanding of the artist's genius.

By the start of the Cinquecento the social standing of the artist had risen so greatly that Raphael and Titian could lead the lives of *grands seigneurs*. And despite the demands of Savonarola that artists should return to their Trecento subservience to theology, no serious attempt was made to control them until the Council of Trent in the middle of the sixteenth century.

BRUNELLESCHI, AND THE EARLY WORKS OF DONATELLO

The competition for the second bronze door of the Baptistery in Florence, organized by the Arte della Calimala (Guild of Cloth-Finishers) in 1401, not only reflects the new economic solidarity of Florence, but also—and more important for our purposes—documents the emergence of the Renaissance style. Of the trial reliefs of the *Sacrifice of Isaac,* the test pieces on which the competition was decided, only two have survived, but the contrast between them is immensely revealing. In Ghiberti's relief (*Ill.* 108) the emphasis is on rhythmic surface patterns extending throughout the entire composition; highly

108,109 *The Sacrifice of Isaac*, by Lorenzo Ghiberti (*left*), and Filippo Brunelleschi (*right*). Both reliefs were executed for the competition of 1401. Bronze parcel-gilt, each 16 in. high.

naturalistic detail is wedded to this structure, and the actual sacrifice is a 'divine pantomime' bearing little relationship to reality. This is totally alien to the new Renaissance nationalism as expressed by Brunelleschi (*Ill.* 109), where the emotional intensity of a real scene is the dominant element. Here the angel intervenes physically to prevent Abraham thrusting the knife into an Isaac who is contorted with terror.

In these two reliefs we are reminded, in that Ghiberti uses a classical torso for his Isaac, of more general principles: firstly that the Renaissance is not merely a revival of classical forms—for these were utilized throughout the Gothic period—but a revival of classical forms in a structure of classical rationalism; and secondly, that a borrowing does not in itself constitute an influence.

Although Brunelleschi was the originator of the new style, Donatello was the great driving force behind its development, and it is from the ideas he exploited that the whole pattern of Florentine Quattrocento sculpture unfolds. His career may be conveniently divided into three periods, the first his early period in Florence, the second from 1443 to 1453 in Padua, and the final period back in Tuscany again until his death in 1466.

During his youth and early period in Florence Donatello's main efforts were directed to increasing the realism and impact of the work of art by reducing the psychological barrier between the work and its beholder. This he achieved by endowing his figures with increasingly strong personalities, as can be seen when the marble *David* begun in 1408 (*Ill.* 110) is compared

110 (*left*) Donatello: *David.* Marble, 75 in. high. Commissioned in 1408 and completed in the following year.

111 (*rignt*) Donatello: *Zuccone.* Marble, 84 in. high. Probably executed between 1427 and 1435/6.

with the *Zuccone* completed in 1435-36 (*Ill.* 111).   The soft,
flowing drapery of the *David* is in contrast to the almost brutal
expressiveness of *Zuccone's* robes, and while *David* mildly con-
templates the middle distance, *Zuccone's* whole personality is
projected at the observer.

The same characteristics appear in Donatello's early reliefs,
with the addition of the scientific perspective he developed in

112 Luca della Robbia: *Trumpeters and Dancing Children*.   Marble relief,
42 in. high. Executed for Florence Cathedral between 1431 and 1438, but
taken down in 1688.

113 Donatello: *St George and the Dragon*. Marble, 15 in. high, executed shortly after 1416-17. Note especially receding arcade on the right.

conjunction with Brunelleschi and the painter Masaccio. The relief of *St George and the Dragon* (*Ill.* 113) under the St George niche on Orsanmichele, dating from shortly before 1420, is the earliest example of a scientifically-planned perspective, and the effect is enhanced by the use of the '*stiacciato*' relief, a pictorial technique of strong modelling in very low relief which he developed to give a greater illusion of depth. The technique is further refined in the Ascension relief of *c.*1430 in the Victoria and Albert Museum, London, and contributes to the triumph of the later Santo reliefs in Padua.

Until he left for Padua in 1443 Donatello completely dominated the Florentine scene, and even Luca della Robbia's reliefs for the Cantoria of the Duomo (*Ill.* 112), notwithstanding their freshness and apparent originality, are heavily dependent upon Donatello's Prato pulpit. The corpus of works he left behind him was a constant source of inspiration and the starting-point for the burst of mid-Quattrocento Florentine sculptural activity.

FLORENTINE SCULPTURE OF THE MID-QUATTROCENTO

Before 1443, Donatello and his collaborator Michelozzo had evolved the earliest of the Humanist tombs. In their fully-developed form, these tombs consist basically of the figure of the deceased dressed in a long silk robe laid out '*al antica*' on a

113

bier over his sarcophagus, set in a tabernacle decorated with a relief of the Madonna and Child, with or without additional reliefs and figures. At the time of the death of the Humanist Leonardo Bruni in 1444 Donatello was in Padua, so that the commission for the tomb went to one of the younger generation, Bernardo Rossellino, who then produced the first fully-developed Humanist tomb (*Ill.* 114, 115). How Bernardo's style had evolved from that of Donatello can be seen by comparing the Bruni tondo of the Madonna and Child with Donatello's relief of the same subject in Berlin (*Ill.* 116). Bernardo's relief is much less

116 (*right*) Donatello: *The Pazzi Madonna*. Marble, 25 in. high. Datable to 1420-22.

117 (*far right*) Desiderio da Settignano: Head of an Angel. Marble, half life-size. *c.* 1461.

114,115 Bernardo Rossellino: Tomb of Leonardo Bruni, S. Croce, Florence. The tomb is undocumented, but work is assumed to have been begun shortly after Bruni's death in 1444 and completed by 1446/7. *Above*: The Madonna and Child tondo from the tomb.

intense, softer, more lyrical, and intimate rather than heroic. This development in Florentine sculpture becomes increasingly pronounced in the tomb of Carlo Marsuppini, who was Bruni's successor as State Chancellor, by Desiderio da Settignano, and in the same sculptor's Altar of the Sacrament in San Lorenzo, where the figures (*Ill.* 117) take on the fragility and elegance of a picture by Filippino Lippi. This style is dominant in Florence until the last quarter of the century, and although it could remain a vigorous force in the hands of Antonio Rossellino and others, it also accounts for the slack figures and sugary sentiments of sculptors like Mino da Fiesole.

The same Humanist desire for the immortality of the individual that had inspired the Humanist tomb also encouraged the revival of the portrait bust and the medal. These classical forms were well known, both through the numerous surviving examples

118 Andrea Arditti: Reliquary bust of St Zenobius, one of the patron saints of Florence. Silver parcel-gilt, life-size. Datable to 1331.

and through literary sources, but the Renaissance evolved a new type of head and shoulders bust derived rather from the medieval reliquary bust than from straight classical prototypes, as can be seen by comparing the silver reliquary bust of St Zenobius by Andrea Arditti of 1331 (*Ill.* 118) with Antonio Rossellino's bust of Giovanni Chellini, signed and dated 1456 (*Ill.* 119).

119 Antonio Rossellino: Portrait bust of Giovanni Chellini, a famous physician in fifteenth century Florence. Marble, 20 in. high, signed and dated 1456.

120 Andrea della Robbia: *The Agony in the Garden*. A characteristic example of an altarpiece executed in coloured della Robbia ware. Figures under life-size.

The great Florentine tradition of sculpture and decorative work in glazed terracotta also emerged in the first half of the Quattrocento, particularly in the production of Luca della Robbia and his family, who gave their name to the medium—della Robbia ware. In Luca's hands it is capable of great subtlety and refinement, as in the decoration of the pendentives of the

Chapel of the Cardinal of Portugal; but later on the possibility of taking many cheap casts from a single model with a minimum of working-up led to almost mass-production methods and an attendant loss of quality. The colours, originally exploited for subtle aesthetic effects, became brighter, often garish, and the technique tended to sink to the level of popular art. The altarpiece in the Louvre (*Ill.* 120) is a good example of these cheerful decorations, and represents a tradition that continues right into the Baroque era.

GOTHIC SCULPTURE AFTER 1400

Before the full ramifications of Donatello's activity in Padua can be explored, reference must be made to the continuing Gothic tradition in Italy and its interrelationship with the Renaissance style. The realistic approach characteristic of fifteenth century Northern Gothic sculpture is also evident in Italy, where it allowed a certain *rapprochement* with the scientific realism of Italian Renaissance sculpture.

After Donatello the greatest sculptor working in Florence in the early Quattrocento is undoubtedly Lorenzo Ghiberti, who, though he drew heavily on Renaissance forms in his later work, always remained a Gothic sculptor in spirit. The total loss of his extensive work in precious metals means that he is now best known as a bronze worker, though like Donatello he also designed cartoons for stained glass windows. For the second pair of bronze doors for the Baptistery in Florence, referred to earlier (see page 109), he follows the lay-out of Andrea Pisano's earlier pair (*Ill.* 122), both in overall conception and in the design of the figure groups filling the fourteen pierced quatrefoils on each door. But Ghiberti exploited the shape of the field much more successfully than Andrea, and in doing so increased the decorative coherence of the ensemble (*Ill.* 121). These doors were completed and installed in 1424. In the third and last pair of doors Ghiberti replaced the quatrefoils by a much simpler system of

118

121 Lorenzo Ghiberti: *Scenes from the Life of Christ, with the Four Evangelists and the Four Fathers of the Latin Church*, decorating the North Door of the Baptistery, Florence. Executed between 1404 and 1424 in bronze parcel-gilt, each panel 20 in. high.

five large square pictorial reliefs on each door, while the frame from which they hang he heavily decorated with lively garlands of foliage, animals, human heads and other highly naturalistic details fully in accord with the Gothic tradition of naturalism. This last pair of doors was not finally installed until 1452, and although the figures are set out in ostensibly scientifically constructed spaces, their graceful swinging folds and the intricate patterns they form belong to the Gothic world of Lorenzo Mo-

122 Andrea Pisano: *Scenes from the Life of St John the Baptist.* Four panels from the North Door of the Baptistery, Florence, executed between 1330 and 1335. Bronze parcel-gilt, each panel 21 in. high.

123 Lorenzo Ghiberti: Two of the Kings waiting to present their gifts to the Infant Christ. Detail of panel 20 in. high, from the door shown in *Ill.* 121, executed between 1404 and 1424.

124 Lorenzo Ghiberti: *The Story of Cain and Abel*. Detail of the Porta del Paradiso (East Door) of the Baptistery, Florence. Bronze gilt, 31 in. square. The door was commissioned in 1425 and completed 1452.

125 Benedetto da Maiano: *The Stigmatisation of St Francis*, reliefs from the pulpit in S. Croce, Florence. Probably executed in the mid-1470s. Marble, 28 in. high.

naco and Fra Angelico rather than to the rational Humanism of Donatello. Nevertheless the pictorial style of these reliefs greatly influenced Florentine relief style of the later Quattrocento, as we see when we compare Ghiberti's *Cain and Abel* (*Ill.* 124) with Benedetto da Maiano's relief of the *Stigmatisation of St Francis* on the pulpit in Santa Croce (*Ill.* 125). Ghiberti's free-standing figures on Orsanmichele (*Ill.* 126) follow the style of the individual figures in his reliefs, and later find a rather anaemic reflection in the early figures of Andrea Sansovino on the Baptistery. Ghiberti really marks the end of the dynamic Gothic tradition in Tuscany, and apart from an extensive, anonymous

126 Lorenzo Ghiberti: *St Matthew.* Bronze, over life-size. Commissioned by the Arte del Cambio for their tabernacle on Orsanmichele in 1419 and completed in 1422.

production of sub-Gothic terracotta and stucco groups of the Madonna and Child derived from Ghiberti compositions, he left little following at his death in 1455.

A position closely comparable to Ghiberti's is occupied by his competitor and the greatest of Sienese sculptors, Jacopo della Quercia. Quercia's earliest undisputed work, the tomb of Ilaria del Carretto in Lucca (*Ill.* 127), probably of 1406, reveals an extremely sensitive style which is still firmly embedded in the late courtois tradition; and again, in the later Trenta Altar in Lucca (*Ill.* 128), completed in 1422, the treatment of relief figures and the architecture as parts of a single unified decorative pattern

127,128 Jacopo della Quercia: *left,* Tomb of Ilaria del Carretto, marble, probably 1406; and *right,* detail of the Trenta Altar, marble, completed in 1422.

129 Jacopo della Quercia: *Zacharias in the Temple.* Gilt bronze relief, 24 in. high, probably executed between 1428 and 1430.

is comparable to carved altarpieces in the North. It is in his bronze relief of *Zacharias in the Temple* (*Ill.* 129) in the Baptistery at Siena that Jacopo comes closest to Ghiberti, like him populating the Renaissance setting with Late Gothic figures. But on the main doorway of San Petronio in Bologna he returned to the heavy drapery style characteristic of the Trenta Altar, and

130 Jacopo della Quercia: *The Creation of Adam.* Istrian stone, 34 in. high. Jacopo's series of monumental figure reliefs on the Porta Maggiore of S. Petronio dates from 1425-35.

produced a series of extremely monumental relief figures that made a deep impression on the young Michelangelo (*Ill.* 130).

This heavy, soft drapery handling is characteristic of much Quattrocento Gothic sculpture, ranging from the elegant marble statuettes by Niccolò dell'Arca decorating the Arca di San Domenico in Bologna (*Ill.* 131) to the vigorous terracottas in the Emilia by Niccolò, Guido Mazzoni (*Ill.* 132) and Antonio Begarelli—an element that points to the influence of Northern Late Gothic sculpture, and more specifically to Burgundian sculpture of the circle of Claus Sluter. The terracottas of Northern Italy were essentially Northern Gothic inspired—in contrast to most of

131 (*left*) Niccolò dell'Arca: A Prophet wearing a turban. Marble, *c.* 20 in. high, probably executed between 1473 and 1494.

132 (*right*) Guido Mazzoni: *The Lamentation over the Dead Christ*. Terracotta, partially pigmented, life-size. The figure is from a *tableau vivant* documented to 1477-80.

those of Tuscany and Central Italy—and the often harrowing realism of the *Pietà* groups is matched in southern Germany and France.

But from this point we may return to Donatello in his second phase, as the great figure in the development of Renaissance sculpture of the late Quattrocento.

DONATELLO IN PADUA AND NORTH ITALIAN CLASSICISM

Donatello left Florence for Padua in order to execute there the new High Altar commissioned for the important church of St Anthony, better known as the Santo. This large-scale composition of both free-standing figures and reliefs was a commission such as was not to be found in Florence during this period, when substantial expenditure was almost entirely confined to building. The Altar was dismantled after 1579, and in its present form is a wildly inaccurate nineteenth century reconstruction. Analysis of all the available data indicates that Donatello rose to the challenge by translating into sculptural terms the newly-developed Florentine pictorial composition—the *'Sacra Conversazione'*. (The *Sacra Conversazione*, or group of saints organized in space round the Madonna, had been invented by Masaccio in his Pisa altarpiece, and developed by Domenico Veneziano in the St Lucy altarpiece while Donatello was working in Florence.) This thesis is supported by the sudden appearance in Northern Italy of a group of *Sacra Conversaziones* of this type by Mantegna, Giovanni Bellini and Antonello da Messina shortly after the execution of the Santo Altar. Here we have an illustration of the extremely close interplay between painting and sculpture—first the translation of a pictorial composition into a sculptural layout, and later the critical influence of Donatello's style in his Santo Altar on that of Mantegna, and on the evolution of North Italian Classicism. For it is in his work on the Santo Altar that Donatello attains his most classical style. The restraint and poise of the Virgin and Child and her silent companions

133 Donatello: *The Virgin and Child Enthroned*. Bronze, 62 in. high. Executed between 1446 and 1448.

leave the excitement of *Zuccone* far away, and show how Donatello has absorbed the essence of classical art and created an image of human dignity hardly attained since classical times. This quality of measured calm pervades the whole complex, reliefs as well as figures, as may be seen in the relief of the *Miracle of the Mule* (*Ill.* 134). In his latest work on the Santo

134 Donatello: *The Miracle of the Unbeliever's Mule which knelt before the Host.* From the High Altar of the Santo, Padua. Bronze, once partly silvered, 22½ in. high. Executed between 1446 and 1448.

Altar, the marble Deposition relief now built into the back (*Ill.* 135), there is revealed a new, much more personal and emotional quality to be exploited by Donatello in his old age.

While in Padua Donatello revived another classical form in the equestrian monument. Here his inspiration was derived not only from the classical bronze horses on the façade of St Mark's in Venice, and the statue of Marcus Aurelius in Rome, but also from the North Italian Gothic tradition as exemplified by the monuments to the Scaligers in Verona. The casting of his over-life-size bronze group of *Gattamelata* was a great technical and artistic breakthrough, and provided the model for Andrea Verrocchio's *Colleone* later in the century.

Donatello must have set up a considerable workshop in Padua in order to carry out the bronze casting and finishing necessary for the completion of the Santo Altar and the *Gattamelata,* and after his departure his assistants continued this tradition with great vigour. Bartolommeo Bellano followed Donatello back to Tuscany, but soon returned to his native Padua, where he worked in a naturalistic style heavily tempered in spirit by Do-

130

natello's classicism, as may be seen in his small bronze statuette of *Europa and the Bull* in the Bargello (*Ill.* 136).

The revival of small-scale free-standing bronze statuettes was a notable contribution of Italian Humanism, and gained momentum during the third quarter of the Quattrocento, particularly in the areas where Donatello had set up bronze-casting workshops. These statuettes had always been highly regarded in classical times, and original examples were eagerly sought after by Renaissance connoisseurs, for, the Humanist desire to live *al antica* apart, these small intimate bronzes opened up new vistas of aesthetic experience, designed as they were to be contemplated, the surface textures to be savoured, and the subtle and often complex planning to be sought out and enjoyed.

Bellano's pupil Andrea Briosco, Il Riccio (died 1532), who really belongs to the Cinquecento, developed from his master's style the synthesis of subtle variations of surface working and infinite ingenuity of design for which he is justly famed. The rich, soft surface modelling, enlivened by brilliant work with

135 Donatello: *The Entombment.* The back of the High Altar of the Santo, Padua. Stone, 54 in. high. This relief was paid for in 1449.

chisel and punch, makes his *Mounted Warrior* (*Ill.* 137) one of the great masterpieces of High Renaissance classicism, and an equestrian monument in miniature. Il Riccio will be mentioned again in the context of High Renaissance Classicism.

If the first major formative influence for North Italian Classicism was the continuance of the bronze-working tradition, the second came not through sculpture directly but through painting. The classicizing ideas present in Donatello's reliefs in the Santo were developed by the painter Jacopo Bellini in his long series of drawings, and this process was carried on by his son-in-law Andrea Mantegna, whose highly classical frescoes in the Ovetari Chapel in Padua (destroyed 1944) were completed in 1459. Mantegna's later, increasingly cool plastic style largely reflects current trends in North Italian Humanist thought, and played an important part in forming the style of such sculptors as the

136 (*left*) Bartolommeo Bellano: *Europa and the Bull*. Bronze, 8½ in. high. Probably made in Padua during the period 1469-96.

137 Riccio: *Mounted Warrior*. Black patinated bronze, 13½ in. high. Almost certainly executed between the completion of the Paschal candlestick in the Santo, 1515, and Riccio's death in 1532; a closer dating is as yet impossible.

138 Il Antico: *Meleager*. Dark patinated bronze parcel-gilt, 12 in. high, datable to the first quarter of the sixteenth century. The companion figure of a boar is lost, but this example illustrates the type of statuette created for Isabella d'Este.

Lombardi, and in particular Il Antico. In the early Cinquecento Piero Bonacolsi, Il Antico, took over and interpreted classical models (hence his name), and the intricate surface working and gilding he lavished on such bronzes as his *Meleager* (*Ill.* 138) panders to the slightly *passé* taste of the highly-sophisticated Mantuan court for which they were created. But in contrast to his contemporary, Riccio, Antico always remained spiritually a Quattrocento artist.

The Certosa at Pavia was for many years the focal point of sculptural activity in Lombardy, and is a veritable museum of Late Quattrocento Lombard sculpture. The vocabulary of classicism derived from Padua was seized upon eagerly by sculptors such as Amadeo, only to be used in a totally unclassical fashion. The façade of the Certosa with its figures and reliefs swamped by a riot of ornamental carving is far closer akin in spirit to transalpine Late Gothic than to the classicism of Padua. Of the many sculptors working on the façade, the most striking are undoubtedly the Mantegazzas (*Ill.* 139), who, while remaining strongly influenced by the Gothic, developed the emotional possibilities inherent in Bellano's handling of the drapery in his *Pietà* relief in the Victoria and Albert Museum, London. Their characteristic 'clinging wet' or 'crumpled paper' draperies evolved from those of Donatello *via* Bellano, but the haggard, gaunt faces owe a heavy debt to North Italian Late Gothic terracottas, as well as to the late Donatello.

In Venice there was the same confused assimilation of the Renaissance, rather than a complete spiritual revolution, for during the course of the Quattrocento she drew heavily on Lombardy for her sculptors. After the middle of the century the rather heterogeneous style of Andrea Bregno, combining a Lombard basis with echoes of Venetian Gothic (*Ill.* 140), was exploited by the Veronese sculptor Antonio Rizzo (d. 1499/1500), whose figures of Adam and Eve (*Ill.* 141) carved for the Doge's Palace after 1483, show this synthesis at its most sensuous.

134

139 (*left*) Cristoforo or Antonio Mantegazza: *A Prophet*. Stone, three-quarters life-size. As yet the Mantegazza brothers cannot be stylistically se-parated, but the statuettes on the façade of the Certosa at Pavia can be dated to the period 1473-89.

140 (*right*) Venetian Gothic School, possibly Giovanni Buon: *The Fall of Adam and Eve*, The Doge's Palace, Venice. Istrian stone, life-size, datable to the decade 1400-10.

141 (*left*) Antonio Rizzo: *Eve*. The Doge's Palace, Venice. Marble, 80 in. high, probably completed after 1491.

142 (*right*) Tullio Lombardo: *Bacchus and Ariadne*. Marble, 22 in. high, probably dating from the early 1520s.

In contrast, during the closing decades of the century a much purer classicizing style, derived from Mantegna, was introduced by Pietro Lombardo through such works as the figures decorating the monument to Pietro Mocenigo. Pietro's son Tullio (*c.* 1455-1532) turned to classical sculpture proper for his guiding force, but the rigidity apparent in his relief of the *Coronation of the Virgin* (1500-02) softens in the following years. His *Bacchus and Ariadne* (*Ill.* 142) shows him at his most lyrical, under the influence of the Humanism of the Gonzaga court at Mantua, where he worked for Isabella d'Este in 1523 and 1527.

Until his death in 1532 Tullio Lombardo and his Quattrocento style remained the strongest force in Venetian sculpture, and the bias he directed, towards a classicism heavily tempered by the hedonism so characteristic of Venetian art and life, was still strong well into the seventeenth century.

After Donatello's return to Tuscany in 1453 the new stylistic elements of his Santo Deposition relief (*Ill.* 135) were intensified, and he evolved a highly emotional and personal late style entirely out of sympathy with Florentine sculptural taste, although through Andrea del Castagno very influential on painting. The bronze relief of *The Lamentation over the Dead Christ* (*Ill.* 143) illustrates how he exploited the emotive possibilities of contrasting worked and unworked bronze, for parts are chiselled, filed, punched, or polished, while other passages are left in the rough-cast state. The project for bronze doors to ornament Siena Cathedral unfortunately never matured, but during his stay in Siena Donatello executed the bronze *John the Baptist* in the Cathedral which shows the full impact of his new style. The

143 Donatello: *The Lamentation over the Dead Christ*. Bronze, height 13½ in.

144 Francesco di Giorgio: *The Flagellation of Christ.* Bronze, 22 in. high. The relief may be dated to about 1478, at the beginning of Francesco's first stay in Urbino.

bronze pulpits of San Lorenzo in Florence were only commissioned as a charity and were completed by Bertoldo after Donatello's death. Their reception can be judged from the fact that they were not set up until the visit of Leo X in 1515, and not until the era of Rosso and Pontormo were these last tortured figures with the flickering ribbons of drapery fully comprehended.

In contrast to the lack of interest of Florentine sculptors in Donatello's late style, Sienese sculpture was revitalized by *John the Baptist* and the projects for the Siena Cathedral doors. Vecchietta's bronze figure of the *Risen Christ* in Siena and Francesco di Giorgio's bronze relief of the *Flagellation* (*Ill.* 144) in Perugia both show not only a considerable debt to Donatello in the subtle use of contrasting surface textures, but also the impact of Donatello's emotionalism on what was still essentially a Gothic ambience. After the Late Quattrocento Siena rapidly declined in importance, until finally she was annexed to Florence by Cosimo I and settled into an artistic backwater.

The sculpture of Agostino di Duccio and his circle falls stylistically outside the area dominated by Donatello and is another facet of the Quattrocento.

Agostino was Florentine by birth, but received his training outside Florence, possibly under Quercia, and executed none of his major works in Tuscany. In the Tempio Malatestiano in Rimini he created a highly individual style where the Quattrocento Renaissance types of the figures are wedded to swinging masses of linear fold patterns, spreading out over the surface of the reliefs (*Ill.* 145). The conscious unreality of these reliefs is further developed in his later work in Perugia, where in his *Miracle of San Bernardino* (*Ill.* 146), completed in 1462 or earlier, the draperies have become like ectoplasm and swirl round the figures in an unearthly symphony. Though these reliefs are among the finest products of the century they remained isolated with little or no following.

Rome in the Quattrocento remained very provincial, and the important commissions available were too few to encourage any major artist to settle there permanently. Some rich patrons looked outside the city, and Donatello and others executed important commissions, either coming to Rome, or working in Florence and exporting the finished product. The only sculptors who stayed for extended periods were secondary figures such as Mino da Fiesole, who had found it unprofitable to compete in Florence and the other great centres, and settled for the quieter if less remunerative life of a provincial centre.

145 Agostino di Duccio: *An Angel drawing back a Curtain*. Marble, under life-size. Agostino was active in the Tempio Malatestiano in the early 1450s.

146 Agostino di Duccio: *A Miracle of San Bernardino of Siena*. Marble, half life-size, executed between 1457 and 1462.

The situation in Naples was comparable, with Francesco Laurana as the principal protagonist. His relief of *Alfonso of Aragon in Triumph with his Court (Ill.* 147) on the arch of the Castelnuovo reveals him as charming, competent, and to a considerable extent heir to the tradition of Late Gothic realism. In Naples as in Rome, however, a great part of the finest sculpture of the Quattrocento is Florentine export work, and ranges from Donatello and Michelozzo's Brancacci monument to the exquisite altars by Antonio Rossellino and Benedetto da Maiano in Sant'Anna dei Lombardi.

The Late Quattrocento in Florence has been left to the end of this discussion, as it was from this ambience that the High Renaissance evolved. As mentioned earlier, Donatello's late style

147 Francesco Laurana: *Alfonso of Aragon in Triumph with his Court*, on the Triumphal Arch of the Castelnuovo in Naples. Marble, half life-size. Laurana's decoration probably dates from between 1452 and 1458.

148 (*left*) Bertoldo di Giovanni: *Arion*. Bronze, 17½ in. high. The figurine probably dates from *c.* 1470-90, and illustrates the type of bronze created for the Medici circle.

149 (*right*) Antonio Pollaiuolo: *Hercules and Antaeus*. Bronze, 17 in. high. Probably executed about 1475-80, and first mentioned in the Medici inventory of 1492.

150 Antonio Pollaiuolo: Tomb of Sixtus IV, St Peter's, Rome. Bronze. The figure of the Pope is slightly over life-size. Commissioned in 1484, but signed and dated 1493.

151 Andrea del Verrocchio: *Christ and Doubting Thomas*. Bronze, over life-size. Commissioned *c.* 1465 and set up in 1483, replacing Donatello's figure of St Louis of Toulouse.

was unsympathetic to most Florentine taste, but the means by which he gained his effects—his refinement of formal layout and of bronze working technique—were extremely potent influences in the evolution of Late Quattrocento Florentine sculpture. Although the sculpture of this period is bewildering in its variety, certain general directions can be detected. After Bertoldo (*Ill.* 148), Antonio Pollaiuolo was perhaps the keenest exploiter of Donatello's techniques, both in his large-scale bronze monuments in Rome to Sixtus IV (*Ill.* 150) and Innocent VIII, and his small-scale bronze statuettes such as the *Hercules and Antaeus* (*Ill.* 149), where he takes over the multiple viewpoint system evolved by Donatello for his *Judith and Holofernes*.

In the large-scale work of the two other most important figures of this period, Benedetto da Maiano and Andrea del Verrocchio, there is a greater feeling for plasticity and a renewed seriousness as the Cinquecento approaches. This is seen in Verrocchio's bronze group of *Christ and Doubting Thomas* on Orsanmichele (*Ill.* 151), executed over the period 1465-82, and in Benedetto's *St Sebastian* of *c.*1495 (*Ill.* 152), whose composed, swelling forms point the way to the High Renaissance.

152 Benedetto da Maiano: *St Sebastian*. Marble, slightly under life-size. A late work left in Benedetto's studio at the time of his death in 1497.

The High Renaissance and Mannerism

The Medici family first emerged as a political power at the time of the revolt of the Ciompi in 1378; and on the death of Rinaldo degli Albizzi in 1434, Cosimo de' Medici, better known as Cosimo il Vecchio, succeeded him as the uncrowned ruler of Florence. The Medici then carried on and developed the control of affairs as it had formerly been practised by the Albizzi: ruling but not being seen to rule. Cosimo circumvented the popular and unworkable constitution of Florence by manipulating the elections so that Medici adherents were invariably returned to the principal offices of state, and then employed the taxation to penalize his political and economic competitors. During this operation he remained a private citizen and so unassailable. And indeed, on the sole occasion that his political adversaries succeeded in having him exiled, the economic effect was so disastrous that they were forced to welcome him back with open arms after only a year.

This breaking of the spirit if not the letter of the Florentine constitution was continued by Lorenzo il Magnifico, Cosimo's grandson, who retreated still further into the political background, passing his time in the family palace in the Via Larga, or at the Villa at Careggi in the company of his neo-Platonic Academy. This Academy, centred round Marsilio Ficino and Pico della Mirandola, was extremely important, both in translating many classical texts into Italian and providing them with commentaries, and in furnishing one of the principal ingredients for the emergence of the High Renaissance and later phenomena of the Cinquecento.

146

The accession of Julius II (della Rovere) in 1503 placed a warrior Pope on the papal throne, the remainder of whose life was dedicated to the consolidation and extension of the temporal power of the papacy. Julius' political failure is in direct contrast to his great success in raising Rome within a few years to a position of artistic pre-eminence that she was rarely to lose until the late seventeenth century. The dynamism of the Pope and the scope offered by the transformation and embellishment of Rome provided two more essential ingredients for the emergence of the High Renaissance.

LEONARDO DA VINCI

As a patron of the arts, Lorenzo il Magnifico is perhaps more remarkable for what he did not do than for what he did, in that apart from Verrocchio and Bertoldo he patronized scarcely a single great artist of the Late Quattrocento and he totally ignored the greatest, Leonardo da Vinci. The problem of Lorenzo's relationship to Leonardo is fundamental. The neo-Platonic emphasis of Florentine Humanist circles must have been an anathema to Leonardo as a lifelong dedicated Aristotelian. These considerations, plus the fact that Leonardo's illegitimacy debarred him from ever becoming a master of the Guild in Florence, and the scarcity of large commissions in Tuscany during the last quarter of the Quattrocento, all made the rich Aristotelian court of the Sforzas in Milan his natural goal, and leaving Florence he stayed there until 1499.

Leonardo represents the culmination of the Quattrocento, in that he was both the greatest flowering of medieval encyclopaedic thought and the epitomy of the Humanist 'uomo universale'— universal man. His vital importance lies in his ceaselessly probing mind, revealed by his writings, drawings and lastly his paintings. To Leonardo the arts had their fullest meaning as processes by which specific intellectual problems were solved: the pursuit of beauty was an intellectual and practical exercise

147

carried out for its own sake and with little regard for its practical applications. This accounts for his extreme reluctance to ever finish a painting once the solution had been reached, and his disastrous habit of experimenting with the medium. But the problems Leonardo set himself to solve as an intellectual exercise and afterwards lost interest in provided a constant source of inspiration for Michelangelo, Raphael and other artists of the Cinquecento, who rationalized and simplified his solutions and then developed the artistic possibilities in them in the terms of the new High Renaissance Classicism. Leonardo's interest in the projected Sforza and Trivulzio equestrian monuments was, one suspects, more experimental than aesthetic, and later monuments through the ages have added few ideas to those he explored for these projects.

NEOPLATONISM AND THE HIGH RENAISSANCE,
HYPERCLASSICISM AND MANNERISM

The transformation from Quattrocento to High Renaissance has its roots in the contrast between Aristotelianism and neo-Platonism. Alberti's concept of beauty in a work of art as the harmony between all the parts so that nothing can be added to it or taken from it without impairing the whole is derived from Aristotle *via* Vitruvius, and is dependent upon the Aristotelian conception of the visible world as ultimate reality. Ficino in his *De Amore* abandoned this position, and using Plotinus, states that 'God, as the totality of goodness, is the centre of the universe, and that beauty is the reflected splendour of this goodness' (P. O. Kristeller); or in other words, that visible external beauty is but a feeble reflection of the invisible beauty of God. From this it follows that the process of creating a beautiful work of art must be from the inside out, since a concept must first be formed in the mind and then be translated into visible terms —a process the direct opposite of the Aristotelian/Albertian one, where the work of art is synthesized by adding together the

148

most beautiful observable examples of the component parts. The latter was Leonardo's approach, while in the High Renaissance view the spirit of classical art inspired and guided the formation of the concept in the mind.

This process of creation from inside out and new relationship to classical art is well seen in Michelangelo's early works, for instance the *Angel bearing a Candlestick* (*Ill.* 153) on the Arca di San Domenico in Bologna, executed during his stay there in 1494-5. Here the figure has a nobility and solemnity quite foreign to the Late Quattrocento, and a new directness, that of a dynamic personality in close relationship to the observer. In the Quattrocento the synthetic process of artistic creation had resulted in a progressive reduction in emotional content with increasing refinement of execution, until in Leonardo's paintings

153 Michelangelo: *Angel bearing a Candlestick*. Marble, 20½ in. high. Bologna, 1494-95.

the figures have immense realism but float in a mysterious dream-world of their own, emotionally divorced from that of the spectator. The figures of Michelangelo and Raphael, on the other hand, have an intense realism, inhabit the same space as the spectator and breathe the same air.

Its very processes of creation make the new style one of idealization, and Michelangelo's *Bruges Madonna and Child* of 1504-5 (*Ill.* 154) has greater poise than his Bologna figure of 1494-5, possessing a certain grave majesty tempered by the warmth and intimacy of the relationship between the mother and her child. The sadly overrated, gangling youths representing *Bacchus* (1497-8) and *David* (1501-04) are painfully immature works in comparison, and only appear at all exceptional because of the almost uniformly indifferent quality of the other sculptors working in Central Italy during the first decade of the Cinquecento, including Andrea Sansovino and Rustici.

In the past Mannerism has almost invariably been treated in terms of a reaction, but this concept will not fit the facts. As Vasari emphasizes when he says that in the young Parmigianino was reborn the spirit of Raphael, contemporaries saw no break, and the sense of continuity in the works is strong. Vasari's concept of *'maniera'* as a positive quality with a precise meaning, to be discussed a little later, is the critical factor in understanding the phenomenon of Mannerism. The course of the evolution of this concept lies in the philosophy of the period and, in particular, in neo-Platonism.

In his *De Amore* Ficino developed the theme that love was to be defined as 'a desire for the fruition of beauty', a *'desiderio di bellezza'*, and that visual experience is merely the first step towards the intelligible and universal beauty reached at the stage of divine love. Pico della Mirandola analyses in detail the stages by which this goal can be reached, comparing them to the rungs of Jacob's Ladder: the first three are, delight in the visible beauty of an individual, idealization of this particu-

154 Michelangelo: *The Bruges Madonna,* Notre Dame, Bruges. Marble, 50 in. high. Commissioned by the Mouscrons of Bruges and delivered there in 1506.

lar visible beauty, and interpretation of it as a mere specimen of visible beauty in general. In his book on manners (*Il Cortigiano*, published in 1528 but worked out in the first decade), Baldassare Castiglione makes Bembo explain these stages to the young prince and elaborate on them. In the first stage he follows Pico straightforwardly, but in the second he elaborated the thesis of idealization, saying '. . . he will bring into his thought so many adornments that, by putting together all beauties, he will form a universal concept and will reduce the multitude of these to the unity of that single beauty which sheds itself on human nature generally.' When Castiglione comes to put the third step into more readily comprehensible terms he compares it to the heightened reality of a vision in a dream or trance, saying 'And thus, instead of going outside himself in thought . . . let him turn within himself, in order to contemplate that beauty which is seen by the eyes of the mind . . . and sometimes when the motive forces of the body are rendered inoperative by assiduous contemplation, or are bound by sleep, then, being no longer fettered by them, the soul senses a certain savour of true angelic beauty . . .'

Michelangelo had lived in the Palazzo Medici in 1493-94 and had come into close contact there with both Ficino and Pico della Mirandola, and Raphael was a close friend of Castiglione, so that these arguments, esoteric though they now appear to us, must have been familiar to both of them, and do much to elucidate the nature of those idealizing tendencies of Cinquecento art which may be termed Hyperclassicism.

From 1508 to 1512 Michelangelo was painting the Sistine ceiling, and in certain of the *ignudi* a new stylistic element appears. The figures take on a cultured elegance and languid grace, with a marked coolness of emotional content (*Ill.* 155). Vasari described this quality in the *proemio* to the third part of his *Lives of the Artists* as '*maniera*'—a term taken over from the language of manners, and in particular from Castiglione, with an absolutely precise meaning. *Maniera* is equivalent to the English 'style', and a person or thing described as possessing style has poise and refinement, or if looked at from the negative viewpoint, unnaturalness and affectation. This quality can be present in people or things at any time—indeed Vasari attributed it to Ghiberti in discussing the Baptistery doors—but the term was in general use in the Cinquecento and usually associated with '*grazia*', grace and '*sprezzatura*' (changed by Vasari in the vocabulary of art criticism to '*facilità*'), the effortless resolution of all difficulties. Michelangelo and Raphael appear to have followed Castiglione's interpretation of Pico's system, and they developed his concept of *maniera* to this end.

152

155 Michelangelo: *Ignudo*. Detail from the vault of the Sistine Chapel, frescoed by Michelangelo in 1508-12.

The new emphasis on *maniera* within the structure of Classicism leads to the phenomen of Hyperclassicism, in which the accent is laid on the qualities of elegance and refinement while retaining the classical vocabulary. The *Ignudo* illustrated above (*Ill.* 155) is a good example of this heightened classicism, as well as of the conscious abstraction and idealization of nature. The subtle distortions of the proportions of the various elements

156 (*left*) Jacopo Sansovino: *Apollo*. Bronze, 58 in. high, executed for the Loggetta, Piazza San Marco, Venice. *c.* 1537-40.

157 (*right*) Sansovino: *Neptune*. Marble, twice life-size, Palazzo Ducale, Venice. Commissioned in 1554 and completed in 1567.

and their relationship throws the whole into sharper focus, and is all part of this quest for heightened reality.   Michelangelo's most explicit statement at this time is his newly developed '*testa divina*', or ideal classical head, which also reflects the development of the quality of *sprezzatura*, for emphasis on the effortless resolution of all difficulties will invariably place a premium on complexity and ingenuity, '*invenzione*', and a certain capriciousness, the '*concetto*' or conceit.   This process led both

154

158 Michelangelo: *The Dying Slave*. Marble, 90 in. high. Begun in 1513 as part of the tomb of Julius II, and after changes in plan presented to François I in *c*. 1546.

to the vigorous exploitation of the grotesque, and to the evolution of the '*figura serpentinata*', that purely aesthetic problem of obtaining the maximum of torsion in the minimum of space. The only reasonable definition of the Mannerist style that can be derived from the foregoing is that it is one which places a particularly strong accent on *maniera* and its attendant qualities.

The abstraction seen in the *Ignudo* from the Sistine ceiling is also strong in Michelangelo's Slaves (*Ill.* 158), executed from 1513 for the tomb of Julius II but never used, which are among the first sculptures produced in the new style. The *figura serpentinata* is much more emphatic in his somewhat unsatisfactory Christ figure in S. Maria sopra Minerva of 1519-20, and the motif became the favourite exercise of figure sculptors for the rest of the century.

THE FIRST HALF OF THE CINQUECENTO

Considered in the framework of the history of sculpture Michelangelo's essential contribution—though not what we today see as his finest work—is his development of High Renaissance Classicism in conjunction with Raphael, and their joint influence in the creation of the Mannerist style in the second decade of the Cinquecento. In 1520 Raphael died, and after the middle of the third decade the highly personal style that Michelangelo evolved had relatively little direct influence on the evolution of Cinquecento sculpture.

Apart from Michelangelo and in comparison with the dazzling developments in painting, sculpture before the Sack of Rome is very disappointing. In Central Italy some of the best productions of this period are the rather dreary classical figures by Andrea Sansovino and his young son Jacopo on the Basso and della Rovere monuments in Santa Maria del Popolo, but they make a poor showing compared to the brilliance and vigour of the Late Quattrocento tradition in Northern Italy, represented by Antico and Tullio Lombardo.

After Michelangelo, il Riccio is undoubtedly the most out-standing sculptor of the first quarter of the Cinquecento, and from Padua he dominated the Veneto until his death in 1532. The reliefs he executed for the della Torre monument in about 1516-21 (*Ill.* 159), now in the Louvre, are the sculptural equi-valents in Northern Italy of Raphael's tapestry cartoons, with which they are almost coeval, and they are among the most explicit expressions of High Renaissance Classicism in all Italy.

The period between the death of Raphael in 1520 and the Sack in 1527 saw the dramatic flowering of the Mannerist style in Rome, and the group of brilliant young artists respon-sible were mostly painters and decorators, including Parmigianino, Rosso, and Raphael's pupils headed by Giulio Romano. The

159 Riccio: *The Death of della Torre*. Bronze, 14½ in. high. Executed in *c.* 1516-20 for della Torre's tomb in Verona, but removed to Paris with its accompanying reliefs by Napoleon.

Sack of Rome by the forces of the Emperor Charles V was the climax of a period of acute political and economic disturbance in Italy, closely connected with the growing strength of the Reformation in Northern Europe; and soon after, the Florentines took advantage of the discomfiture of the Medici Pope, Clement VII, to eject the Medici family once again and set up a Republican government. The city only capitulated after a long siege by the Medici forces, ending in 1530, and in the next decade her financial condition was not such as to be able to support any extensive sculptural activity, other than Michelangelo's work in the Medici Chapel.

The Veneto alone in Italy remained relatively stable during these upheavals, and Jacopo Sansovino left Rome after the Sack to pass most of the rest of his life there, bringing with him Roman High Renaissance Classicism. He remained faithful to this style right up to his death in 1570, though when his late works are compared to the figures on the Loggetta of 1537-40 (*Ill.* 156), a certain softening and new warmth under Venetian influence is evident, as in the *Giants* decorating the staircase of the Doge's Palace (*Ill.* 157).

It came about because of the supremacy of classicism in Venice during the first half of the Cinquecento, and the unfavourable political and economic conditions elsewhere in Italy in the third and fourth decades of the century, that the first major sculptural commissions executed in the Mannerist style were outside Italy—at Fontainebleau. Once François I had rid himself of his disastrous military ambitions he became an enormously enthusiastic patron of the arts, and endeavoured to entice Italian artists to France. Leonardo accepted his offers and died in France in 1519; Andrea del Sarto stayed there briefly in 1518-19, and Michelangelo sent several figures while declining to leave Italy. But after the disasters of the third decade the prospect of working in France became very much more attractive to Italian artists. Rosso arrived there in 1530, followed by Primaticcio in 1532, and Cellini paid a visit in 1537 and returned for five years in 1540-45. The great cycles of stucco decorations created by Rosso (*Ill.* 160) and Primaticcio at Fontainebleau have no real precedent, but the elongated figures with their languid poses, and the richness of the *invenzione* carry forward the ideas of the late Raphael, particularly as developed by Parmigianino.

The ideas embodied in the Fontainebleau decorations were brought back to Rome for the decoration of the Sala Regia in the Vatican and later complexes, and lay the foundations for the very vigorous tradition of Roman stucco-work that continues into the eighteenth century.

During his second stay in France Cellini executed the *Nymph of Fontainebleau*, now in the Louvre (*Ill.* 161), in which he

160 Rosso Fiorentino: *Ignudo* from the Galerie François I at Fontainebleau, decorated in 1533-40. Stucco, slightly under life-size.

translates the stucco style of Rosso and Primaticcio into bronze with the further refinement of his training as a goldsmith.

With the close of the fourth decade there was a renewal of intense sculptural activity in Central Italy, and the key to this lies largely in the revival of the financial fortunes of the Medici family and their re-emergence as the major secular art patrons in Central Italy. Michelangelo had left Florence in 1534 with the Medici Chapel almost finished, and despite the pressure brought to bear on him by Cosimo I, refused to return. In his absence the sculptors Tribolo and Montorsoli evolved for the Medici Villa Castello outside Florence some of the earliest of the fully-developed Renaissance fountain complexes (*Ill.* 162), and from that time onwards the decoration of the fountain provided one of the major outlets for sculpture.

The emphasis of the Mannerist style on grace, elegance, wit and ingenuity made it very unsatisfactory for religious art, and attempts to retain the forms while replacing the elements of

161 Benvenuto Cellini: *The Nymph of Fontainebleau.* Bronze, over life-size. Executed in 1543-44 for Fontainebleau.

162 Niccolò Tribolo: Fountain of Hercules and Antaeus. Bronze and marble. Designed for the Villa Castello, near Florence, by Tribolo, and executed by various sculptors after 1536.

invenzione and *concetto* by intricate allegorical symbolism, such as may be seen in the paintings of Vasari and the sculpture of Baccio Bandinelli, were doomed to failure. While in purely secular sculpture, and in particular in the medium of bronze, the Mannerist style remained vigorous and satisfying until well into the seventeenth century, the sense of conflict and increasing theorizing sapped almost all its strength when it was applied to serious commissions to which it was not suited. Vincenzo Danti's Muses and the *Brazen Serpent* (*Ill.* 164) illustrates the opposite outcome of this antipathy between style and subject,

163 Pierino da Vinci: Detail from the Fountain of Hercules and Antaeus, Florence, illustrated on the previous page.

164 Vincenzo Danti: *Moses and the Brazen Serpent*. Bronze, 32 in. high. Executed for Cosimo I, probably in 1560-61.

165 Michelangelo: *Pietà*. Intended by Michelangelo for his own tomb, and first mentioned in 1550 by Vasari. The polished areas that spoil the left-hand side are the responsibility of Tiberio Calcagni. Marble, height 89 in.

because though it is a superb work of art, its religious significance is almost nil. Michelangelo died in 1564 after years of worship as 'Il Divino', but his highly personal late style as seen in the Florence Cathedral *Pietà* (*Ill.* 165) was totally unintelligible to his contemporaries, and they had to look elsewhere for a way out of the impasse religious sculpture had reached.

163

The last session of the Council of Trent closed in 1563, but the future policy of the Roman Catholic Church towards the arts had been made known some years earlier. Extremists at the Council had been strongly opposed to the visual arts on principle, but the moderates had triumphed, and laid down a series of instructions for artists so that the visual arts should serve the Faith for the purposes of propaganda. These demands included simplicity, clarity and intelligibility, as well as the avoidance of the nude—all principles opposed to the cultivation of *maniera*—but they showed the way out of the impasse and eventually to the Baroque. How far, in the atmosphere of neo-medievalism of men such as Molanus, the codifiers of these demands had in mind the realism of Late Gothic art is an open question; but given their instinctive dislike of classical ideas, and the power of still-medieval Spain looming large behind the Council, this interpretation is probably correct.

The greatest sculptors of the second half of the Cinquecento, and in particular Giambologna, were capable of working in both the Mannerist and what may be termed the Counter-Reformation Realist style, adopting whichever better suited the commission in hand, so that until the advent of the Baroque we have the co-existence of two equally valid styles. This is a phenomen comparable to the co-existence in the previous century of the Quattrocento Renaissance and Gothic styles, and as before, there is a somewhat diffuse division between the two.

The middle of the century also marks the beginning of the extensive programme of embellishment of Florence that transformed it into the city we know today, and the quantity of sculpture executed in the next half century or so was truly prodigious. Cellini continued to employ the Mannerist style with great brilliance in the *Perseus* he completed in 1554 (*Ill.* 166), and the wealth of *invenzione* he lavished on the base (*Ill.* 167) illustrates well the Florentine love of the capricious and grotesque. It was as a part of the same rather haphazard programme that Ammanati executed the heavy, lumpish marble figure of Neptune for the fountain outside the Palazzo Vecchio, and further decorated it with a superb series of bronze figures (*Ill.* 168) that carry on admirably the finest traditions of Mannerism. Giambologna emerges from this ambience and pursues a very similiar style in the bronze figure of *Apollo* he executed in 1573-75 for the study of the second Grand Duke, Francesco I.

Born in Douai in 1529, Giambologna was one of the great number of Northern painters and sculptors who poured into Italy in the second half of the Cinquecento, and after his first appearance in the competition for the Neptune fountain, won by Ammanati, he rapidly became the strongest personality among the sculptors of Central Italy. His enormous studio

166,167 Benvenuto Cellini: on the left, *Perseus with the Head of Medusa.* Bronze, 126 in. high. The figure was commissioned in 1545 and set up in 1554, and the difficulties met in its casting are vividly described in Cellini's autobiography. *Right:* detail of the pedestal, marble and bronze, *c.* 60 in. high, showing the statuettes of Danae and Jupiter and the exotic grotesques.

168 (*left*) Bartolommeo Ammanati: *Marine Goddess*. Bronze, over life-size, c. 1571-75. A subsidiary figure on the Neptune Fountain, Florence.

169 (*right*) Pietro Francavilla: *Winter*. Marble, over life-size. One of a set representing the Seasons, executed in the 1590s for the Ponte S. Trinità, Florence.

included such sculptors as Francavilla (*Ill.* 169), Tacca and Susini, and lasted until well into the seventeenth century providing a potent source of inspiration for French and German sculpture of the late sixteenth and early seventeenth centuries, as well as for Italian sculpture. The increasing power and movement of his compositions can be followed from the Neptune Fountain in Bologna 1563-7 (*Ill.* 170), through the *Rape of the Sabine* completed in 1582 (*Ill.* 171), to the *Hercules and the Centaur* of

166

170 *(top left)* Giambologna: *Neptune*. Bronze, *c.* 152 in. high, from the Fountain of Neptune, Bologna. The figure was cast in 1566.

171 *(top right)* Giambologna: *The Rape of the Sabine*. Marble, 161 in. high, signed and dated 1582.

172 *(lower left)* Giambologna: *Hercules and the Centaur*. Marble, 106 in. high, signed and dated 1600.

1594-99 (*Ill.* 172), where the proto-Baroque tendencies of his late style are strongly apparent. In the last group his movement away from the grace and elegance of the Mannerist style and into the realism of the Early Baroque is complete—a development also seen in the reliefs on the base of the equestrian monument to Cosimo I completed in 1599.

This pattern of development is typical of many Central Italian sculptors, but in Venice the Counter-Reformation never made the same impact as it did in Rome or Florence, possibly because of the action of the Venetian Senate in outlawing the Jesuits in their territory. The Mannerist style was developed by Danese Cattaneo in such figures as those decorating the Loredano tomb, completed in 1572, or the little bronze *Fortuna* in the Bargello (*Ill.* 173), but in Venice the style never reaches the same pitch of elegance and refinement as in Florence. The old contrast between Venice and Central Italy, that of '*colore*' versus '*disegno*'—in other words, between compositions built up in terms of light and colour and those built up in terms of line and expressive silhouette—continues to apply, even if one of the most Mannerist of Venetian figures, the *Fortuna*, is taken for comparison with Cellini's *Perseus*.

Alessandro Vittoria (1525-1608) occupies a position in Venice parallel to Giambologna's in Florence, and developed a powerful style based on the mature works of his master Jacopo Sansovino and on a close study of Michelangelo's Louvre *Slaves*, as is apparent in his tentative early statue of *St Sebastian* in San Francesco della Vigna, which is almost a pastiche of Michelangelo. The Louvre *Slaves* proved a constant fascination to him, and even as late as his *St Sebastian* in San Salvatore of *c.*1600 he looks to the *Rebellious Slave*. He was, however, a far finer modeller than carver of marble, and the *Neptune with a Sea-Horse* (*Ill.* 174) reveals him as the heir to the subtleties of surface handling of Riccio, while he imbues the figures with truly Michelangelesque movement.

The Venetian Renaissance is carried on into the seventeenth century in the small bronze statuettes of Tiziano Aspetti (died 1607) and Niccolò Roccatagliata (died 1636), which are often charming (*Ill. 175*), though totally devoid of the vitality so characteristic of Vittoria.

In Rome the Counter-Reformation took on a stern note, and the uncompromising natures of such Popes as Paul IV and Sixtus V are reflected in the dry, prosaic figures and reliefs decorating the tombs in the Sistine Chapel in Santa Maria Mag-

173 (*left*) Danese Cattaneo: *Fortuna*. Bronze, 19¾ in. high, mid sixteenth century.

174 (*centre*) Alessandro Vittoria: *Neptune with Sea-Horse*. Bronze, 20 in. high, probably *c*. 1580-85.

175 (*right*) Niccolò Roccatagliata: *Bacchus*. Bronze, 17 in. high, early seventeenth century.

176 Giambologna: *Marching Soldiers*. Bronze, detail approx. 12 in. high, from the relief of *Cosimo I triumphant over Siena* on the base of the equestrian monument to Cosimo I, Florence. Executed 1595-9.

giore, by the Lombard Valsoldo and the Flemings Gillis van den Vliete (Egidio della Riviera) and Nicolas Mostaert (Nicolo Pippi). At their worst these sculptures often degenerate into pure propaganda, but the style takes on a new dignity at the very end of the century in the hands of sculptors such as Nicolo Cordieri and Pietro Bernini, when it merges into Early Baroque.

Baroque and Rococo

THE EARLY BAROQUE: MOCCHI

During the pontificate of Paul V Borghese (1605-21), sculpture lagged behind painting, and there was little comparable to the pictures of Annibale Carracci and Caravaggio. Borghese patronage in the first and second decades of the seventeenth century tended always to be somewhat conservative, as we can see from the major sculptural complex of the period—the decoration of the Pauline Chapel in Santa Maria Maggiore in Rome. Here the layout of figures and pictorial reliefs closely followed that of the Sistine Chapel, which it balances in the church, but the architectural elements of the huge wall tombs of Paul V and Clement VIII entirely swamp the flaccid, colourless sculpture and emphasize its essential timidity.

The Farnese family, that of Pope Paul III, were far more advanced in their patronage, and in commissioning Annibale Carracci to decorate the Gallery of the Palazzo Farnese, Cardinal Odoardo Farnese had introduced to Rome the Bolognese painters whose classicism dominates the Roman scene in the second decade.

In this atmosphere Late Renaissance Classicism remained a reasonably valid sculptural style, having reached a passable standard of quality in the work of such sculptors as Nicolo Cordieri and Pietro Bernini; and it passed into the Early Baroque in the late works of Camillo Mariani, such as the figures of saints in San Bernardo alle Terme in Rome (*Ill.* 177), and the early work of Francesco Mocchi, as represented by the *Annunciation* figures (*Ill.* 178) from Orvieto Cathedral (1603-8).

The most striking quality of Mocchi's figures is their clarity and simple directness; they have none of the empty rhetorical

177 (*left*) Camillo Mariani: *St Catherine*, San Bernardino alle Terme, Rome. Stucco, over life-size, 1600.

178 (*right*) Francesco Mocchi: *Angel of the Annunciation*. Marble, over life-size. Executed for Orvieto Cathedral in 1605.

gestures of much Mannerist art, and so illustrate admirably the Counter-Reformation demands for intelligibility and realism. Mocchi's next great work, his bronze equestrian monument to *Ranuccio Farnese* of 1612-20 at Piacenza (*Ill.* 179), not only demonstrates the advanced nature of Farnese patronage but is also something of a voice crying in the wilderness, heralding the arrival of the High Baroque. The handling of the reliefs on the base, on the other hand (*Ill.* 180), continues to look to Bolognese classicism.

172

179,180 Francesco Mocchi: The Equestrian monument to Ranuccio Farnese, bronze, over life-size, executed 1612-20; *left*, detail of the *Allegory of Good Government* on the base of the monument. Bronze, detail *c.* 12 in. high.

The characteristics of the Baroque are concentration on the creation of as close a personal relationship as possible between the work of art and the observer—and so a rejection of the thesis of ideal abstraction favoured by the Renaissance—and an often extreme sensuality in the pursuit of realism. This approach finds its religious parallel in St Ignatius Loyola's 'Spiritual Exercises', in which the worshipper is called upon to imagine the torments of the Passion of Christ inflicted on his own body. To the modern observer Bernini's figure of *St Theresa* (*Ill.* 181), as it were frozen into marble at the climax of a self-induced orgasm, is acutely embarrassing, but to the seventeenth century such a triumph of realism was perfectly valid in that it inspired the observer to share in the ecstacy of the saint. This sensuality runs right through the century, even after the second quarter when classicism begins to reassert itself.

181 (*left*) Gianlorenzo Bernini: *The Ecstasy of St Theresa*. White and coloured marbles, over life-size. 1644-52.

182 (*right*) Bernini: *The Rape of Proserpine*. Marble, 96 in. high. 1622-5.

Mocchi's statue of *Ranuccio Farnese* with its tremendous *brio*,
the rippling movement through the draperies of the young prince
and the sensuous modelling of the horse's flanks and its soft,
flowing tail, is in startling contrast to Giambologna's almost
hieratical equestrian statue of *Cosimo I*, unveiled in 1598, and
really only finds a parallel in the equestrian portraits of Rubens
and Van Dyck. The equestrian monument, like any other
statue that has to stand isolated, must have multiple viewpoints,
but the claim of the great nineteenth century art historian Wölfflin
that this is a characteristic of all Baroque sculpture is totally
misleading. In fact almost the opposite is true, for in its
pursuit of clarity and realism the seventeenth century rejected the
multiple viewpoints of the Mannerist sculptors where possible in
favour of the single principal viewpoint with the maximum
impact on the observer.

183 (*left*) Gianlorenzo Bernini: *Apollo and Daphne*. Marble, 96 in. high.
1622-5. The subject is taken from Ovid's Metamorphoses.
184 (*right*) Bernini: *David*. Marble, 67 in. high. 1623.

If Francesco Mocchi heralded the High Baroque, he was rapidly eclipsed by the new star rising at the beginning of the third decade—Gianlorenzo Bernini, the giant of the Italian Baroque. While his father, Pietro Bernini, was working in the Pauline Chapel the young prodigy caught the attention of Paul V, and more important—that of Paul's nephew Cardinal Scipione Borghese. He entered the Cardinal's service in 1617, aged only nineteen, and remained there until 1624. Rome dominates the artistic scene in Italy for the first three quarters of the seventeenth century, and during this, the heroic period of Baroque patronage, the pattern evolves around the successive popes and their families. Cardinal Scipione Borghese was one of the most lavish patrons of the century, and in the few short years that he worked for him, Bernini produced a series of monumental groups in which can be plotted his lightning development.

The *Rape of Proserpine* (*Ill.* 182) exploits with great energy the rather cool beauty of Annibale Carracci's figures on the Farnese ceiling, while the *Apollo and Daphne* (*Ill.* 183), begun in 1622, portrays the precise moment at which Daphne, touched by Apollo, turns into a laurel tree. This portrayal of a clearly-defined instant in time is a characteristic of the Baroque, but the *Apollo and Daphne* has the immature fragility of two children playing at life and totally lacks the punch of the last of the groups—the *David* of 1622 (*Ill.* 184). This last has the same instantaneous quality—but here David is depicted at the point of releasing his sling, and his figure is extremely menacing as he glares directly at the observer, who realizes that he is in the place of Goliath. To heighten the realism and thus the impact of these figures Bernini systematically developed a very subtle textural handling of marble, well shown in the *Apollo and Daphne*, and this he derived from his great source, other than the Farnese ceiling: Hellenistic Greek sculpture; or more precisely, Roman marble copies after Hellenistic Greek

185 Gianlorenzo Bernini: The Baldacchino and Cathedra Petri, St Peter's, Rome. Bronze, partly gilt. (see pp. 179, 184).

186 (*left*) Gianlorenzo Bernini: *St Longinus*. Marble, *c*. 15 ft high. St Peter's, Rome. Like the Baldacchino (previous page), executed for Urban VIII.

187 (*right*) François Duquesnoy: *St Andrew*. Marble, *c*. 15 ft high, executed for Urban VIII. St Peter's, Rome.

bronzes. These Hellenistic works also exerted their influence on form, and such *mouvementé* Hellenistic marbles as the Belvedere torso and the *Laocoön*, greatly admired in the sixteenth century, now came fully into their own. Michelangelo had followed up the Baroque ideas inherent in them in certain passages of the Sistine ceiling, such as the *Crucifixion of Haman*, but had gone on to develop the hyperclassical style of Mannerism, so that these much-lauded statues had exerted remarkably little direct influence on the sculpture of the sixteenth century.

In 1623 Maffeo Barberini ascended the papal throne as Urban VIII, and with great ruthlessness and excellent taste inaugurated the Baroque embellishment of Rome. The completion of the decoration of St Peter's was to occupy most of the century, and from the start Bernini was at the centre of the plans of the Pope and the innumerable Barberini Cardinals. The Baldacchino (*Ill.* 185) was begun in 1624 and *St Longinus* in 1629—the year Bernini was appointed 'Architect of St. Peter's'. The figure of *St Longinus* (*Ill.* 186), depicted at the moment of conversion, is characteristic of the High Baroque in its enormous energy and dynamic equilibrium. The great diagonal sweep of his outstretched arms is controlled by the impetuously gathered up draperies pulled across his body, while the cascade of the cloak falling from his right shoulder counterbalances the upward thrust of the slender shaft of the spear. But despite the tremendous vitality and exuberance of the whole composition the vital message, 'Truly this was the Son of God', remains to the fore, and in this respect the High Baroque can be said to be the greatest expression of the Counter-Reformation.

BAROQUE VERSUS CLASSICISM, AND ALESSANDRO ALGARDI

The years around 1630 saw the crystallization of the controversy of Baroque versus Classicism that was to continue to rage, on and off, during most of the rest of the century. This controversy was mainly between painters, and hinged on whether a scene should be depicted with the minimum of figures, following classical theory, or with many figures, on the grounds that a painting, like an epic (according to Pietro da Cortona), should have a principal theme and many subsidiary episodes. This led in turn to the argument as to whether the painting should appeal to the senses—the hedonistic principle of delight as a *raison d'être*—or only to the intellect, and these two approaches are directly reflected in the sculpture of the period.

The painter, architect and designer of stuccoes Pietro da Cortona led the Baroque faction with Bernini, while the painters Andrea Sacchi and Nicolas Poussin championed the classical cause together with the Flemish sculptor François Duquesnoy,

188 Gianlorenzo Bernini: *The River Nile*. Detail of the Fountain of the
Four Rivers, Rome. The Nile is depicted with his head shrouded as the
source of the river was then unknown. Marble, twice life-size, executed by
G. A. Fancelli from a modello by Bernini in 1647-51.

who lived in Rome during 1618-43. This did not mean, however, that the Baroque party ceased to subscribe to classical art theory; rather that Bernini and Cortona emphasized different facets from those emphasized by the classical party. This difference is admirably illustrated by their drawings after classical sculpture, as Cortona's interests are in Hellenistic and Imperial Roman sculpture, while Poussin's drawings are mainly after Republican Roman pieces.

This phenomenon of High Baroque Classicism is to a certain extent a continuation of the Bolognese Classicism of the second decade, but it is now a matter of theory, not merely of taste, and the doctrine becomes progressively more rigid with time—especially after the foundation of the French Academy in 1666. Duquesnoy's figure of *St Andrew* (*Ill.* 187) stands in St Peter's opposite Bernini's *St Longinus*, its contemporary, and the comparison between the two is most revealing. Both figures are unquestionably Baroque, but, in contrast to the dynamic composition of the Bernini, Duquesnoy's figure is absolutely static and posed; even the heavy and slightly over-elaborate draperies are completely motionless. Duquesnoy's statue of *Santa Susanna* (*Ill.* 189) of the same years is even more restrained and classical while clearly betraying his Northern training, and the soft, rotund *putti* for which he is most famous belong firmly to the world of Rubens and Van Dyck, and strike a strangely alien note in the Roman churches.

Apart from Duquesnoy, the only sculptor of rank to remain independent of Bernini was Alessandro Algardi, who at first took up a position between the extremes of Baroque and Classicism, as we see in his figure of the *Magdalen* (*c*.1628) in S. Silvestro al Quirinale in Rome.

After the disastrous First War of Castro, beginning in 1641, and the death of Urban VIII in 1644, the Roman Giambattista Pamfili became Pope, as Innocent X, and threatened to inquire into the financial affairs of the Barberini, who had left the papacy hopelessly in debt. Urban's relatives fled from the city, and with them were discredited all the artists who had been closely associated with them, including Bernini. Algardi's opportunity had come, and his great contribution to the High Baroque, the relief of the *Meeting of Leo I and Attila* (Ill. 190), was commissioned by Innocent X for St Peter's in 1646. The relief, almost 25 feet high, was completed in 1653, the year before his death, and shows a compromise between the Grand Manner as expressed by Bernini and his own classicizing tendencies. The treatment of the highly dramatic subject is remarkably restrained, and this coolness is further emphasized by

189 (*left*) François Duquesnoy: *S. Susanna*. Terracotta, life-size, 1626-33. S. Maria di Loreto, Rome.

190 (*right*) Alessandro Algardi: *The Meeting of Leo I and Attila*. Marble, St Peter's Rome. This huge relief was Innocent X's principal contribution to the decoration of St Peter's, executed 1646-53.

191 Pietro da Cortona: Decorative stuccoes in the Palazzo Pitti, Florence. Partly gilt. 1643-5.

the smooth, evenly-worked marble, which is in direct contrast to Bernini's differentiation of texture and sparkling surfaces. The relief was the prototype for a great series of sculpted altarpieces which replaced painted altarpieces in the second half of the century whenever circumstances permitted.

BERNINI, 1644 - 1680

During the early pontificate of Innocent X Bernini was able to undertake his first large private commission since the accession of Urban VIII—the Cornaro Chapel in Santa Maria della Vittoria with the group of the *Ecstasy of St Theresa* (1644-52, *Ill.* 181). This chapel is one of the finest flights of High Baroque illusionism, with the marble group floating like a white jewel surrounded by richly-coloured marbles, and flooded with light pouring down gilt bronze rays from a concealed source—a device that reminds us of Bernini's activity as a theatrical designer.

Bernini's increased interest in colour in sculpture, realized by the use of variegated marble and gilt metal, was shared by the other great artist of the Barberini entourage, Pietro da Cortona. Pietro left Rome to live for several years in Florence in the mid-1640s, where he painted the ceilings of a series of rooms in the Palazzo Pitti and designed the exuberant white and gilt stuccoes that surround them (*Ill.* 191). These works in the 1640s point the way to the next pontificate, with Bernini's *Cathedra Petri* and Gaulli's decoration of the vault of the Gesù.

Bernini returned to papal favour with the completion of the *Fountain of the Four Rivers* (*Ill.* 188) for the centre of the Piazza Navona, the nexus of Pamfili patronage. But although the Pamfili rapidly came to acknowledge his artistic pre-eminence in Rome, he did not succeed in regaining his position of artistic dominance until Fabio Chigi became Pope Alexander VII in 1655.

In Bernini's late works the elements of colour and directed light become increasingly important, and the techniques exploited in the *St Theresa* are developed on a gigantic scale in the *Cathedra Petri* (*Ill.* 185). Here four great bronze figures carry the bronze shrine containing the sacred chair, while above a blaze of gilt-bronze rays and angels radiate from the yellow glass window bearing the Dove. The structure completely fills the space between the pilasters, and as the worshipper enters the basilica, his eye is led through the structure of the Baldacchino and the rising smoke of the candles to this sunburst of 'divine' light hovering behind the High Altar.

Gaulli's *Adoration of the Name of Jesus* painted in 1674-9 on the nave ceiling of the Gesù under the supervision of Bernini carries the process one stage further, and the observer is left wondering where the painted figures stop and the Berniniesque white and gold stuccoes take over; but the future of such extreme Baroque illusionism lay not in Italy, but in Germany in the hands of the Asams and others.

After the death of Alexander VII in 1667 there was a sharp decline in papal patronage, though this was to a certain extent offset by increased patronage from the Jesuits and other Counter-

Reformation Orders, whose financial position had improved sufficiently by the second half of the century for them to embark on a massive programme of church decoration. The turn of the last quarter of the century also saw renewed activity in the Baroque versus Classicism controversy, with the aged Bernini backed by Gaulli in opposition to Sacchi's pupil Carlo Maratta—but by this time the whole controversy had shifted in the direction of the Baroque and the productions of the two parties were much closer together. Bernini had attempted a *rapprochement* with the classical party in the 1630s, with not entirely happy results, but in his late works such as the Beata Lodovica Albertoni or his bust of Gabriele Fonseca these is a restraint and depth of introspection not seen in his more Baroque work. This change is also evident when Bernini's tomb of Urban VIII (*Ill.* 192), executed in 1628-47, is compared with that of Alexander VII (*Ill.* 193), executed 1671-8. The drama-

192, 193 Gianlorenzo Bernini: *Left,* Tomb of Urban VIII, executed 1628-47; *Right*, Tomb of Alexander VII, executed 1671-78. Both white and coloured marble and bronze, figures over life-size.

tic figure of Urban depicted at the monument of his blessing *'Urbe et Orbi'* is replaced on the second tomb by the composed kneeling figure of Alexander deep in prayer. These two tombs are immensely influential in that until well into the eighteenth century, they supplied the models for almost every papal tomb as well as for those of innumerable lesser fry. The increased strength of classicism can to a certain extent be equated with the increasing French influence in Rome, particularly after the foundation of the French Academy there in 1666, though the extreme classicism of Duquesnoy and Poussin found no direct successors.

While in painting Rome declined from her position of dominance in the last quarter of the seventeenth century and the provincial centres grew more important, in sculpture she remained the fountainhead until well into the eighteenth century.

194 (*left*) Melchiorre Caffà: *The Ecstasy of St Catherine*. White and coloured marble, figure over life-size. Completed 1667.

195 (*right*) Ercole Ferrata: Detail of *The Stoning of St Emerenziana*. Marble, figures over life-size. The relief was begun in 1660, and the upper section completed over the twenty years following Ferrata's death by L. Retti.

196 (*left*) Antonio Raggi: Allegorical figures. Stucco, over life-size, executed 1669-83. Detail of the Clerestory of the Nave of the Gesù, Rome.

197 (*right*) Filippo Carcani: Decorative figures. Stucco, over life-size, *c.* 1685. S. Giovanni in Laterano, Rome.

THE LATE BAROQUE

The overall pattern of development of sculpture in the late seventeenth and early eighteenth century is very complicated, but three broad streams can be detected, with the Sicilian Giacomo Serpotta remaining a law unto himself. The first stream depends from Bernini and includes Caffà, Raggi and Carcani; the second arises from Algardi, leading to Ferrata, Rusconi, Foggini, Soldani, Mazza and their successors; the third lies entirely outside Rome and includes sculptors like Parodi and Corradini.

The Maltese Melchiorre Caffà (1635-1667/8) was a pupil of Ercole Ferrata, but in his short working career of a little over a decade he leaned towards Bernini. In his *Ecstasy of St Catherine* (*Ill.* 194) he succeeded in transforming the dynamic power

187

of Bernini's *St Theresa* into a much more restrained and picturesque Late Baroque idiom. The extremely sensitive surface differentiation is dependent upon Bernini, but in contrast to *St Theresa* where the spectator drawn into sharing the passion of the saint, St Catherine's ecstasy and intense nervous energy are entirely personal, and even the attendant angels are distant observers.

Antonio Raggi (1624-1686) was trained under Algardi, but after joining Bernini in the mid-1640s he became his most intimate and prolific pupil. His finest works are his stuccoes, and under the wing of Bernini he collaborated with Gaulli in the decoration of the nave of the Gesù (1669-83, *Ill.* 196), where his agitated figures, articulated by great zig-zag masses of drapery, develop Bernini's style of the Chigi Chapels in Santa Maria del Popolo and Siena Cathedral. But no matter how complex his figures are, Raggi never loses sight of the basic structure of flesh and bones that carries the drapery, while his follower Filippo Carcani, whose work mainly dates from 1670-90, loses interest in structure and evolves a proto-Rococo style with elegant figures wrapped round with parallel masses of drapery. His stucco figures decorating the Lancellotti Chapel in S. Giovanni in Laterano (*Ill.* 197) reflect current movements in ceiling painting: the various elements of the figures are organized mainly with regard to the overall decorative effect, and relatively little attention is paid to the organic unity of the individual figures. It is not entirely surprising that such a revolutionary view of the function of sculpture failed to find any immediate following in the prevailing classical atmosphere, and Carcani is mainly interesting as a prophet.

The second main stream of development depends from Algardi, transmitted *via* Ferrata. The Lombard Ercole Ferrata (1610-1686) worked under Bernini in St Peter's and then veered towards Algardi's compromise classicism, as may be seen by comparing his relief of the *Stoning of S. Emerenziana* in S. Agnese (*Ill.* 195) with Algardi's of *Leo and Attila* (*Ill.* 190). Ferrata has

198 Camillo Rusconi: *St Matthew.* Marble, over life-size, 1713-15. Nave of S. Giovanni in Laterano, Rome.

composed his relief according to the classical precepts, with the minimum of figures divided into clearly defined groups according to the part they play in the action. He has renounced Bernini's surface differentiation of the marble and here adopts Algardi's even surface working. The result is extremely competent, but, compared with the brilliance of his pupil, Caffà, rather dull.

After the turn of the century Camillo Rusconi (1658-1728) was the strongest artistic character among sculptors in Rome. At first a pupil of Ferrata, he derived much from Raggi and then turned in the same direction as Carcani; but finally, under the impact of Maratta, he evolved what has been best described as

189

199 (*left*) Pietro Bracci: *Neptune*, from the Fontana Trevi, Rome, designed by Nicola Salvi. Marble, over life-size. The lower figures of the fountain-complex were executed between 1759 and 1762.

200 (*right*) Filippo della Valle: *Temperance*. Marble, over life-size. *c.* 1735. S. Giovanni in Laterano, Rome.

the Heroic Late Baroque Classical style. His monumental figures decorating the nave of S. Giovanni in Laterano (*Ill.* 198) have tremendous dynamic power, but they are wrapped up in them-selves, and in their calm assurance and soft even handling they are the heirs of Algardi rather than the late Bernini.

Filippo della Valle (1697-1770) and Pietro Bracci (1700-1773) transformed this style into a Classical Rococo, where the heroic and dynamic qualities of Rusconi are replaced by the tenderness and lyricism so characteristic of the 'Age of Sensibility'. Bracci's exuberant and somewhat theatrical *Neptune* (*Ill.* 199) on Nicola Salvi's Fontana Trevi admirably illustrates the change from Ber-nini's style, while Filippo della Valle's figure of *Temperance* (*Ill.* 200) reveals the strong influence of French sculpture and in particular of the highly-refined sensuality of the Louis XV period.

Florence in the last years of the seventeenth century and the first quarter of the eighteenth was the scene of considerable sculptural activity, led by Giambattista Foggini (1652-1737) and Massimiliano Soldani (1658-1740), who were both pupils of Ferrata. Foggini was a first-rate marble sculptor, as is attested by the bust of Cardinal Gian Carlo de' Medici (*Ill.* 201), but both these sculptors are chiefly important for their small-scale bronzes, which rapidly spread far and wide over Europe, and were particularly influential in Germany. The tradition of small-scale bronzes in Florence, as represented by Giambologna, had remained vigorous, and the Tacca and Susini families had produced casts from his models for most of the century. Foggini's *Flaying of Marsyas* (*Ill.* 202), dated 1716 and inscribed as being a gift from the Grand Duke Cosimo III to the French painter Rigaud, is ex-

201, 202 Giambattista Foggini: *Left*, Bust of Cardinal Gian Carlo de' Medici. Marble, 41½ in. high, datable to the last quarter of the seventeenth century. *Right*: Foggini's *The Flaying of Marsyas*. Bronze, 24½ in. high. The inscription is dated 1716.

203 Giacomo Serpotta: *Charity*. Stucco, approximately life-size, *c.* 1735. Oratory of S. Lorenzo, Palermo, Sicily.

204 Luigi Vanvitelli: Groups of *Diana and Actaeon,* from the Great Cascade at Caserta, near Naples. Marble, slightly over life-size, *c.* 1770.

205 (*left*) Antonio Corradini: Allegorical figure of *Modesty*, marble, over life-size, in the Capella Sansevero de' Sangri, Naples. Executed during 1749-52. The handling somewhat belies the ostensible subject.

206 (*right*) Francesco Queirolo: Allegory of *Deception*, marble, over life-size, also from the Capella Sansevero de' Sangri. Executed during 1750-62.

tremely advanced for its date as compared with Rome, showing developed Rococo tendencies a decade or so before Filippo della Valle or Bracci.

Soldani is a direct contemporary of Rusconi and stylistically very close to Foggini, though his modelling, in the Seattle *Mourning over the Dead Christ* for example, is less taut and his draperies are more elaborate. Giuseppe Mazza (1653 - c.1741), the last of this group of sculptors, practised an extremely restrained Late Baroque Classicism—eventually owing its inspiration to Algardi—working in Venice and Pesaro as well as in his native Emilia.

In fact it is outside Rome that the Italian Rococo reaches its finest flowering, developing from the Late Baroque of such works as the much-maligned Cappella Sansevero de' Sangri, to

193

the brilliant stucco decorations of Giacomo Serpotta in Sicily and Luigi Vanvitelli's fountains in the Park at Caserta (*Ill.* 204).

The decoration of the Cappella Sansevero de' Sangri was mostly carried out between 1749 and 1766—by Antonio Corradini (*Ill.* 205) until his death in 1752, and then by Francesco Queirolo, 1704-1762 (*Ill.* 206) and others. The style of these exceedingly rich and chaotic decorations is one of unrelieved virtuosity, with figures struggling out of marble fishnets or swathed in all-revealing shrouds and other such conceits. Such hypertrophic virtuosity is the ultimate development of the surface differentiation that had so absorbed Bernini, and was to continue to fascinate sculptors like Raffaele Monti (*Ill.* 207) in the nineteenth century.

207 Raffaele Monti: *Veiled Woman.* Marble, 13¾ in. high. Exhibited at the Great Exhibition of 1851.

THE BEGINNINGS OF MODERN SCULPTURE

The Mid Sixteenth to Mid Seventeenth Centuries

We have treated the Northern Renaissance in the first part of this book as an extension of Gothic, and have chosen to mark a main division in the second quarter of the sixteenth century, where the style variously termed Mannerist or Late Renaissance comes in. It is at this point that we see the advent in the Northern countries of an approach to sculpture which may properly be termed modern, since whatever stylistic changes take place, its fundamental principles continue until the most recent contemporary movements.

From the mid sixteenth century onwards sculpture is representational and naturalistic in the broad sense of the term. It is normally based on the human figure and is dependent on human emotions or incidents for its expression and subject matter. This was, of course, also the case to some extent for Gothic, but the handling of the figures now ceases to be stylized and impersonal. The Renaissance Humanist approach is adopted, and independence of personality is demanded even for carved figures. The sculptures are no longer type representations—heads, hands and feet and robes—but, at least when carved by artists of distinction, individuals of flesh, blood and bones, each reacting in accordance with his or her own personality.

Even religious sculptures, which had hitherto served to remind the beholder of the venerated person or holy story largely by means of attributes, now expressed the artist's personal interpretation of these subjects, and set out to impose that interpretation on the viewer. Even the allegorical figures—virtues, vices or heroes—so popular in the sixteenth and seventeenth centuries, appear as individuals imbued with particular attributes rather than as mere formal stock representations of the abstract qualities. It is perhaps necessary to qualify these remarks by pointing out that they apply only to the best work, and that over this period in the North, artists of outstanding quality were not very numerous.

Perhaps the greatest innovation from Gothic is the increasing emphasis on the physical beauty of the models. This is all-important, and nude or clothed, they tend to show themselves to their best advantage. At first the approach is almost always chaste, and in the North it is not until the eighteenth century that sex-appeal is much exploited.

During the following centuries all sculptural styles owe their origins to Italy, while Italian sculpture in turn derives its inspiration from classical sources, though 'classical' in this context implies Imperial Rome rather than Greece of the fifth century B.C. Almost every piece of sculpture—like every picture—'tells a story'. Whether contained in a single figure or a narrative relief, that story is usually perfectly straightforward and clear, at least in its presentation. If the subject or its implication are not immediately recognizable today, this is probably due to a lack of the religious or historical knowledge then common, rather than to any obscurity in the rendering. This approach is of course in direct contrast to most recent contemporary styles and to much primitive carving.

The break from Gothic was undoubtedly due as much to political and social factors as to any current artistic influence. First and most important of these factors was the triumph of the Reformation in many Northern countries. Second, there were the effects of the firm establishment of autocratic, central monarchies and principalities: the courts and capitals became important for patronage, and upon the development of states in the modern sense there followed local patriotism and support for local talent. These factors were not wholly encouraging to the arts, and certainly for sculpture in the North this period

196

was one of decline. Religious sculpture, which had been the main outlet for the art since the twelfth century, was cut off at a single stroke in areas which adopted the new faith, by the iconoclasm of the Protestant reformers. Only sepulchral monuments and to a lesser extent portraits continued to offer any notable market. Even decorative sculpture, which was at first usually associated with and even subservient to architecture, was limited, for the really elaborate work on houses and gardens did not begin to be at all widespread in the North until the latter part of the seventeenth century.

In laying emphasis on the immediate practical effect of Protestant iconoclasm we may be telling only half the story, for the reformers' whole philosophical and emotional swing towards simplicity was surely just as important as their religious disapproval of carved icons. This Puritan manifestation, which was basically an extension of the old Gothic idealistic morality, permeated throughout the North, even in areas where the new Church was never officially accepted, or where, as in France, it was accepted for but a short period.

The division between North and South—or rather North and the Mediterranean—noted in the case of Gothic, never completely dies out. Despite the great Italian impact on style, the detached, Platonic bias of Northern sculpture continued throughout the sixteenth century, and fundamentally even through the Baroque of the next hundred years. Even the sculptures of Catholic Flanders in the seventeenth century brought nothing to compare in sensual exuberance with the paintings of Rubens.

Indeed, in the sixteenth century something of the Northern spirit seems even to have penetrated southward into Italy, where normally the richer and more Aristotelian qualities continued to prevail: there is a considerable difference between the Tuscan innovations of the Quattrocento and the work of the highly-intellectualized later Italian classicists of the Cinquecento. While the classicism of the Florentine Renaissance had been outstandingly successful in its cultivated sensuality, many works of the later sixteenth-century Italian sculptors, especially from Rome or Venice, seem awkward, and as if they had rather unwillingly subscribed to their intellectual restraints.

How the Renaissance and Mannerist styles in the North derived from the Italian sources is generally fairly clear, but a distinction must be drawn between the adoption of ornament and details by the workshop type of sculptors and the much more complete assimilation by the court artists. Such decorative motifs as pilasters, acanthus, classical mouldings, torcheres, *putti* and the like were quite readily disseminated by the paintings or sketch-books and engravings which had always existed, and which were to have increasing influence down the centuries. Small objects like bronzes and boxwoods may also have played a part.

The Northern sculptors of the first half of the sixteenth century no doubt owed something, too, to direct personal contact with Italian work, through the Southern artists working in the North. Since the first years of the sixteenth century several centres had possessed works executed by Italian artists. There were, for instance, the royal tombs by Gaggini and others at St Denis, Torrigiano's monument to Henry VII in Westminster Abbey in London (*Ills.* 208, 209), his later work in Spain, and Michelangelo's Bruges Madonna, which had been available since the first decades of the sixteenth century. Casts were also known, though they do not seem to have been common. Though such pieces by Italian sculptors were at first rare and not immediately influential, their curiosity value must have been considerable, and their effect on the younger and less conservative sculptors correspondingly great. By the mid-century the greatly increased number of Italian artists active in the North—including Cellini working at Fontainebleau and Sansovino and others in the Iberian peninsula—completed the work.

At the opening of the period it was still fairly unusual for any but a few individualist sculptors to travel to Rome for study, but by the second half of the sixteenth century the practice of seeking training in Italy had become well established. Thereafter it became almost the rule for artists of note to spend at least a year or two in the peninsula. The culmination of this movement was the seventeenth-century establishment of schools and academies in Rome by foreign nations.

The Northern assimilation and modification of Italian influences at the outset—and also the effect of Northern sculptures on the visiting Italians—is nowhere better demonstrated than in the Church of San Panteleon at Troyes. The figures show clearly the Italian modification of the Northern idiom (*Ill.* 211), and we can see the gallicizing of the Italian style in a group (*Ill.* 210) reasonably attributed to the Italian Domenico Fiorentino, who had settled in this last traditional Gothic stronghold of Burgundy. Here the exactness of the Northern observation of detail,

208, 209 Pietro Torrigiano: Details from the monument to Henry VII in Westminster Abbey, London. Bronze, approximately life-size, 1512-18.

a great contribution of Late Gothic painting, has produced a tautening of the Italian sensuality.

Seen against this background of Italian influence the sculptors of the sixteenth and even seventeenth century tend to fall into two broad categories: first there were those—the numerical majority—who continued in the old guild and workshop tradition, attached to their locality; and second, those who set themselves apart as independent artists in the new tradition, often travelling far afield and working as commissions offered. But even within these categories things were changing. The workshop was more often an independent family business, passed on from father to son, or for that matter, to widow or other heir, as much on a basis of proprietorship as artistic capacity. The same was the case for lesser architects and painters under the Guilds. These artist-groups joined together in a revolt against the medieval artisan-craftsman status, to form a class somewhat apart—an artistic intelligentsia—which sought to take on something of the Italian artist's position in society. Intermarriage was frequent, whether for reasons of business convenience or like thinking, and the association between groups served to maintain a solid basis for the arts. The workshops undertook the more ordinary commissions and also provided a training ground for new talent. Inevitably they tended to be conservative, and throughout Northern Europe the older styles of sculpture, modified and adapted perhaps, but still clearly traceable, continued even into the seventeenth century.

Yet if this tradition lay behind the mass of the works, by far the most interesting sculpture and stylistic developments are naturally to be found in the work of the leading individualist artists, working in the new classical-Italianate manner. These depended almost entirely on the courts for patronage.

As Mannerism in Italy had evolved within the highly-civilized courts, and was designed to provide for their delectation, it is not surprising that its appeal to the North was as a court art, and that

210 (*left*) Domenico del Barbiere, called Domenico Fiorentino: *Charity*. Painted stone, second quarter of the sixteenth century. S. Pantaleon, Troyes.

211 (*right*) St John the Baptist. Painted stone, second quarter of the sixteenth century. S. Pantaleon, Troyes, France.

in the main it was confined to court circles. Its concentration on the artificiality, graces and elegancies of privileged life naturally recommended itself more highly and found more ready acceptance in the palaces than in the still-feudal castles of the provincial nobility, or in the soldier-burgher homes, although elements of the new style penetrated even these in the course of time.

A feature of this new patronage was that the court taste, though nominally governed by that of the sovereign, was in fact inevitably dependent on the royal advisers, who played an increasingly important part in deciding what artists or style succeeded. Again following the Italian lead, as the artist came

201

up in the social world so patronage came to be regarded as a status symbol, and to be expected of any with pretensions to be advanced. In this way the commissioning of works of art began to occupy a more important place in cultivated life.

In Protestant areas the main outlet for sculpture was the personal monument, and particularly tombs in churches. Naturally such creations were only possible for the rich and privileged, and were in consequence conceived in the exaggerated taste of the privileged at the time, and designed to express their apartness. The effigies were no longer the crusading soldier or noble knight lying dead in his armour, but represented the deceased in life, generally in elaborate robes of office and kneeling, standing, or reclining. They were a perpetuation of superiority over the rest of the world, and inevitably accompanied by a portentous narrative of the deceased's virtues and benefactions, written in Latin which only the few would know. Similarly with the public statues of ruling princes: although these were intended for the masses to gaze upon there is no attempt at anything fundamentally popular in approach or conception, as had been the case in Gothic art. In these as on the sepulchral monument the practice was to present the subject as someone apart, usually wearing classical costume, parade armour or some other badge of culture and distinction.

If such public expressions reflect the social trends of the day, it is perhaps the new lay sculptures which show the most remarkable combination of current artistic influences: Renaissance Humanist sensuality, the classical heritage, the new realism and later the Counter-Reformation theatricality. Though comparatively few at first, these sculptures were destined to play an increasingly important part, until they finally came to dominate the academies of the seventeenth, eighteenth and even nineteenth centuries. In complete contrast to the reasonableness of medieval carving, we now find everywhere members of the pagan classical pantheon, parading the streets and squares or in the homes and gardens of the rich, gesticulating unrealistically, nude or nearly nude. The conception might have made some sense in midsummer Greece, but was curiously ill-adapted to a cold climate; yet it was to become the criterion of cultivated taste and aesthetic appreciation for several centuries.

In Catholic areas the religious sculptures pressed into the service of the Catholic Counter-Reformation became extremely influential after the Council of Trent. While retaining a classical basis, they adopted all the emotional extremes of theatrical illusionism, designed to draw the beholder almost physically into the scenes portrayed. The saints with their sufferings and martyrdoms became increasingly popular as subjects for religious representation, and the approach of sculpture as a whole takes on a new realism. Whether in the figures of Christ on the Cross, the Madonna or the saints and martyrs, the interest is in the physical suffering for humanity, rather than in the Christian statement as in Romanesque, or in divine love as in the Gothic and Early Renaissance. The school of hyper-naturalism which grew up as a reflection of the contemporary religious approach in Italy, and particularly in Spain, has continued for the ordinary church sculptures right up to the present day. In opposition, church sculpture in the Puritan areas became more and more restrained, till scarcely a carved leaf or a moulding was allowed to relieve the Spartan austerity of their world.

One of the most successful and notable types of work of the mid sixteenth to seventeenth centuries, especially in Germany and Flanders, was the *Kleinplastik* (the small intimate sculptures designed as works of art). Curiously enough, medal designs seem to decline in quality.

At this point we shall consider the sculptures under the headings of national schools to which—as variants of the general theme—they came to conform, for the fierce local and individual pretensions and loyalties of the new courts and nations were not without their influence on sculpture. The old universality of the medieval Church, which had played so important a part in maintaining a unified development in the early periods, had come to an end, and local stylistic developments became marked according to the personalities of the leading artists or patrons of the area.

FRANCE

After the political and religious disturbances of the fifteenth and early sixteenth century had died down and the emergent nations had taken firmer shape, France was fortunate in that, although the next hundred years were far from trouble-free, her dynastic and religious difficulties had a less wholesale effect on the arts than

212 Germain Pilon: Caryatids for the urn which contained the heart of Henri II. Marble, mid sixteenth century.

those of other countries. She also had a series of rulers who were really interested in the arts. At least two of her kings, François I and Henri IV, two notable cardinals who also ruled the country, Mazarin and Richelieu, and at least one queen, Catherine dei Medici, were exceptionally civilized patrons, under whose influence culture and the arts prospered. Even the intervening courts were not positively inimical, as was sometimes the case elsewhere, so that the centre always managed to take a lead in the promotion of sculpture and patronage of the better and more individualistic artists. For the rest, as elsewhere in the North, a modified traditional school persisted for the execution of the bulk of the work.

213,214 Jean Goujon: *left*, Monument to Louis de Brézé, marble, mid sixteenth century; and *right*, two nymphs from the *Fontaine des Innocents, Paris.* Stone, mid sixteenth century.

The true beginning of the new influence is marked by the palace buildings of François I—especially Fontainebleau, where artists such as Rosso and Primaticcio, and slightly later Cellini, promoted a fashion for the new Italianate style. It was largely through these artists that Mannerism grew up in France. Sometimes wealthy officers of state, or commercial centres such as Troyes (pages 199-200) encouraged the new mode, but the development as a whole was a court art. At first the sculptures were markedly subservient to architecture, and the painterly inspiration was not absent, as it was basically from the stucco works and caryatid figures accompanying the painted decorations on ceilings, walls or fireplaces that the Mannerist influence spread. Exceptional works such as the great doorway at Anet can only have fanned the flame. From these influences, assimilated and developed by the leading artists, a style grew up that was to dominate France for the next century, and whose influence was to continue long beyond that.

The most notable of the earlier leading sculptors are perhaps Jean Goujon and Pierre Bontemps. These contemporaries are also interesting as representatives of the two parallel streams of tradition, and the new directions that sculpture was to take. The new Italianate classical approach was well represented in Goujon, albeit in a very French interpretation, while the persistence of the more traditional elements is apparent in Bontemps.

At the outset Goujon himself paid service to the past, as we see in the monument to Louis de Brézé, c.1540 (*Ill.* 213), which still owes much to the traditional northern Flemish handling of architecture, figures and details. But the reliefs from the *Fontaine des Innocents* (*Ill.* 214) some ten years later, and the works which follow it are in the full classical taste. Notable are the caryatid-type figures adapted from the stucco decorations which were to become so marked a feature of French sculpture (*Ill.* 215), and persist with modest variations up to the present century. Bontemps, on the other hand, shows himself even in the tomb

215 Jean Goujon under Primaticcio: Stucco decorations for Fontainebleau. Mid sixteenth century.

of François I, around 1547, as a sculptor in the rather more robust, conservative taste. Though his work is less clumsy and rigid than that of many of his provincial contemporaries, it nevertheless lacks the grace that marks the more advanced sculptures of the century.

Slightly later, in the 1560s, the greatest of the new sculptors appears: Germain Pilon (1534-1590). Pilon was indeed the outstanding genius of this whole period in France. The main movements of the day can nowhere be better observed than in his work, and particularly in the great series preserved at the Louvre. Pilon, though young, had advanced so far by the 1560s that he was entrusted with the commission for a receptacle for the heart of Henri II (*Ill.* 212), and for this he produced one of his most enchanting works. Here we see the French caryatid motif at its happiest. The elegance, poise and balance that Pilon has given to what otherwise might have been a rather hackneyed presentation make it an outstanding work of art, in which is blended the best of the French and Italian. Two years later, under the direction of Primaticcio, we find him at work on the astonishing monument to the King and Catherine dei Medici. This is not only one of the stranger philosophical statements of royalty, but one of the world's major masterpieces of sculpture. Here Pilon shows himself working in at least two entirely different manners, neither of which is associable with that of the receptacle. Above, the figures of the King and Queen are represented kneeling in prayer, and rendered in a way that emphasizes the Italian influence and recalls sober court portraiture in the most impeccable royal taste, such as Leoni's figures at the Escorial. But on a platform below the King and Queen lie naked, portrayed as cadavers (*Ill.* 216). This is Northern. The idea of the cadaver

216,217 Germain Pilon: cadavers from the monument to Henri II and Catherine dei Medici, St Denis, near Paris. Marble, third quarter of the sixteenth century, and *below*, relief from the monument to Valentine Balbiani, wife of René de Birague. Marble, last quarter of the sixteenth century.

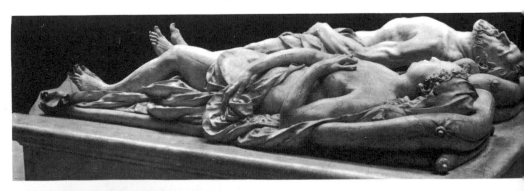

was Gothic, and though it was fairly rare, an example was to be found on the neighbouring tomb of François I. But as rendered by Pilon it is fascinating both as a demonstration of religious feeling and sign of the confidence the monarchy must have felt in its position to admit such personal, worldly fallability. The experiment was not often repeated on the tombs of the nobility. In this curious, dramatic and sensitive handling we find another facet of Pilon, and one in which he is as superb as in any of his styles.

Twenty years later, in 1583, Pilon was to repeat the cadaver theme on the monument to Valentine Balbiani (*Ill.* 217), wife of the Chancellor René de Birague. The treatment here is closely related to that of the royal figures, though possibly a little more acidly dynamic. On the same monument comes yet another style in the splendid Italianate relief of the *Deposition* (*Ill.* 218). On the slightly later monument to the Chancellor himself (*Ill.* 220) we find another kneeling figure in robes. Pilon's French and personal development in 'fining down' is apparent in all these sculptures. The naturalistic yet formal interpretation of the figure of the Chancellor was to set the fashion for many decades.

218 Germain Pilon: *The Deposition*. Bronze, last quarter of the sixteenth century.

Allied with this monument, at least in style, is the group of splendidly refined portrait busts. However much these may owe to Italian sources, the intensely personal handling makes them important in their own right as a tribute to Pilon's versatility and genius. Also belonging to the 1580s, and executed as part of a commission for the Queen, is the exquisite terracotta *Virgin* (*Ill.* 219). This recalls if anything the lyrical late French Gothic style exemplified in the Toulouse Madonna (*Ill.* 73). The interpretation of French tradition and classical and Italian themes reached a truly remarkable culmination in Pilon, whose influence was to continue right down the centuries. Even Rude adapted directly from him in the nineteenth century.

After the death of Pilon no sculptor of equal standing emerges. Indeed the period, coinciding as it did with the height of the

219,220 Germain Pilon: *left*, The Virgin. Terracotta, life-size, end of the sixteenth century. *Right*: Detail of the kneeling figure of René de Birague. Bronze, third quarter of the sixteenth century.

religious wars, was not such as to encourage artists of significance. Simon Guillan (1581-1658), though Italian-trained for a short time and influenced by Pilon, stands like Bontemps or the new King's sculptor, Barthelmy Prieur, for the rather heavier traditional approach. Slightly more distinguished among the sculptors of the early seventeenth century was Jacques Sarrazin (1588-1660), whose caryatids and monuments provide a decent continuity of the classical manner. While paying suitable tribute to Roman associations, they are firmly Northern in their somewhat frigid finality. Sarrazin himself was Protestant. Similarly, the contemporary sculptors Michel and François Anguier carry to the Louvre something of Algardi and Cortona. Mixed with the formal French classicism, their influence created a style which was to last until the new interpretations that come with Versailles in the latter half of the century. It is the medallist and sculptor Jean Warin, if anyone, who brings some intimacy to this rather severe scene of classical casts or classical interpretations.

Apart from the work of these leading individualistic sculptors there is only the rather pedestrian continuation of the guild and workshop tradition. An interesting example of such continued production is to be seen in the ambulatory screen of the cathedral at Chartres, begun early in the sixteenth century and continued intermittently throughout two centuries without very noticeable departure from the original style.

It is curious, in view of the great Paris tradition of the fourteenth century and the courtly domination in arts and crafts, that there is scarcely any production of high-quality intimate objects, whether in ivory or bronze or boxwood. There were, for instance, the series of bronzes by the Anguiers (*Ill.* 221) and also many wood reliefs and figurines of surprisingly high quality for the sixteenth- and seventeenth-century furniture, but small-scale work such as flourished in Germany or Italy seems to have found little encouragement in France. This is even more surprising when we consider that bronzes after the antique or those of artists

211

221 (*left*) Michel Anguier: *Ceres*. Bronze, 22 in. high. Mid seventeenth century.

222 (*right*) Pierre Puget: *Milo of Crotona*. Marble, life-size, third quarter of the seventeenth century.

such as Giovanni Bologna were frequently imported. At the mid-seventeenth century Girardon himself had a large collection.

What is true of Paris and the north of France is less true of the south. There at this time, as earlier and later, the tendency was rather towards an association with Italy. Even so it was not until Puget (*Ill.* 222), later in the seventeenth century, that we find work of any great notability appearing in the south.

THE LOW COUNTRIES

The effects of Protestant iconoclasm over the period were perhaps even more disastrous for sculptors in the Low Countries than elsewhere, since the Reformation naturally cut deeply into the mass export market for religious carvings, the mainstay and

stimulus of the sculptor's guilds since the latter half of the fifteenth century. Later, in the seventeenth century, sculpture was
also adversely affected by the economic and political issues aris-
ing from the Spanish domination, here complicating the universal struggle between the reformed and established faiths. But at
the outset the chief and most immediate problem was the virtual
cessation of the export trade in altarpieces and religious carvings.

So strong were the guilds and so great the number of trained
workmen seeking an outlet that considerable efforts must have
been made to find new directions for their activity. Some religious carving was still needed to serve the Catholic areas, but the
guilds were quick to supplement these by exploiting the new taste
for architectural sculptures and tombs on the one hand, and
Kleinplastik on the other. There was, besides, a commercial
development to meet the new taste for carved figures and panels
on furniture. The long-established training and traditions of the
Low Countries were well adapted to these ends.

As a further contribution to solving the difficulty, craftsmen
as well as works were sent abroad, and throughout the North,
and especially in Spain and England, Flemish carvings and Flemish sculptors continued to play an important role.

But if these changes of direction served to sustain the sculptural tradition out of which better things were to come, the
present aesthetic quality of the production left much to be
desired. Even such earlier refinements as the charming ballet
stylizations of the late Antwerp groups were abandoned in favour
of a pedestrian adaptation of graphic Italian classicizing naturalism. Taken no doubt in large part from prints, the new styles
were rendered in three dimensions in a way that the Italian
Quattrocento would scarcely have accepted. While the figures
may have been recognizably presented and the groups arranged
according to the principles of the new approach, the whole tended
to become a purely narrative statement, and there was little attempt to create a work of art in which the overall form and line

provided the artistic excitement. As far as there was any embellishment, it was usually a lumpy exaggeration of ornamental details, such as embroidery or jewellery, or a rather misunderstood simplification of the main lines of the drapery. The idea that the individual elements should all be co-ordinated into an aesthetic whole seems to have passed these sculptors by. Even with the better masters such as Cornelis Floris (*Ill.* 223) or Pieter Coeck, the workshop conception predominates. This is well illustrated by the famous tabernacle at Leu, where tier upon tier of reliefs and statuettes are set into a wedding-cake architectural construction some thirty or forty feet high. This conception may have as its source the elaborate architectural housings of the late Gothic altars, but now the multiplication of the individual sculptures and their placing has made them almost completely invisible, so that the whole is of little interest unless for its technical elaboration and ingenuity. The same criticisms apply

223 Cornelis Floris: *Christ carrying the Cross*. Detail from the Rood Screen, Tournai Cathedral. Marble, *c.* 1570.

224 The Last Supper. Mantelpiece in the Town Hall, Antwerp.

to the monuments where the architectural whole is the main
point of interest. The effigies or attendant allegories are seldom
of any great distinction, and such contribution as these objects
make depends on the relationship of black touch and white
marble, and the richness of elaborate decoration.

If such works as these set the main direction of sculpture,
there were also, no doubt continuing from the export traditions,
a host of small mass-produced wood or alabaster reliefs. These
were designed to be made up into house altars and votive tablets,
or—with lay scenes—to be used by the joiners in the decoration of caskets or furniture. Together with larger architectural
adjuncts such as mantelpieces and doorways they continued to
be exported throughout the sixteenth century. The fireplace
(*Ill.* 224) is typical of the type of work. Even if such works
were not all Flemish in origin they were of Flemish inspiration.

Of greater sculptural merit was the commercialized *Kleinplastik*. This was fairly widespread in its development, and statuettes of saints and Madonnas, crucifixes and reliefs in boxwood or ivory are found all over the Continent. Besides the religious carvings there were secular ivories with figures or reliefs, often carved as drums for the decorated tankards which had a considerable vogue by the end of the seventeenth century, mounted as show pieces in silver or gilt metal (*Ill. 225*). Although at this period of a wide interchange of design it is unwise to insist on a direct Flemish origin in every case, the majority of these objects seem to derive from Flemish inspiration and sources, or to have been produced abroad by Flemish artisans.

Unfortunately for the Low Countries it was not only the ordinary artisan who emigrated, but most of the more notable sculptor personalities of the sixteenth century as well. First and foremost was Giovanni Bologna, who left at the age of fifteen

225 Bernard Strauss: Tankard of ivory with silver-gilt mounts. Signed and dated 1651. Height 19 in.

never to return, and whose work must really be accounted Italian; later Adrien de Vries and Hubert Gerhardt left to study in his workshop and remained abroad, so that they can scarcely be regarded as Flemish sculptors. Many of the more modest exponents, too, like the Colts and the Cures who came to England, or Collijn who went to the South, are really to be looked upon as artists of the countries of their adoption.

But the paralysis of tradition was not to last for ever; by the seventeenth century fresh winds had begun to blow, and some work was produced of very respectable quality—though not perhaps of the superlative standard of contemporary painting. There are no sculptors of a genius to match Rubens or Van Dyck from the south, or Rembrandt and the great train of seventeenth century painters from the Dutch territories.

Such advance as took place may well be credited to the final Catholic triumph in the south. The internal affairs of the Low Countries at the time were extremely complicated, and it is perhaps sufficient for our purpose to mention again that here as elsewhere the Reformers and Catholics had disagreed, and that the religious cleavage was further aggravated by the dominion of Spain. Though it was not to be officially recognized until later, an uneasy solution was reached with the *de facto* establishment of a Protestant area occupying roughly what is now Holland, under the House of Orange, and of an intensely Catholic Flanders, in which all opposition was virtually crushed by the time of the Archduke Albert and the Regent Isabella (the daughter of Philip II, who had been given the Low Countries as dowry on her marriage in 1596). From then on the Counter-Reformation triumphed in the Spanish areas, and under its influence and encouragement, and deeply influenced by its greatest exponent in painting, Rubens, a school of sculpture evolved which lasted almost through the eighteenth century. For Flanders, therefore, it is rather arbitrary to mark a break in the middle of the seventeenth century, as we have done in the case of other countries.

In the early seventeenth century one sculptor stands out: François Duquesnoy (1594-1643). Though most of his work was done abroad (*Ills.* 187, 189) his influence was all-important, especially as transmitted through his son and pupil, Hieronymus II, and his pupil Artus Quellinus (1609-1668). Between them these two artists laid the basis for Netherlandish sculpture of the late seventeenth and eighteenth centuries. Like most other sculptors at the time, both were members of families who had followed the same profession for generations. This family continuity and workshop inheritance, noted earlier, was always important in European art, and particularly in the Netherlands.

In the Dutch territories the Protestant bias had done little to encourage sculpture, and while work on tombs and monuments persisted it was of no great significance. Only Hendrik de Keyser (1565-1621) stands out as one of the better sculptors in a traditional style. The flowering of great genius in painting seems to have left little room for excellence in sculpture, and indeed when in 1650 the Burghers of Amsterdam wished for some modest decoration for their new Town Hall, they turned to Antwerp and invited Artus Quellinus to do the work.

GERMANY

That the output of sculpture in Germany declined markedly after the great period of the earlier sixteenth century is not surprising in view of the Reformation and the internal disturbances and wars. Apart from the work of a few artists, most of them born outside Germanic territory, the sculpture of the second half of the sixteenth and the seventeenth century became as pedestrian as that of England, and such developments as there were within the German states continued along traditional lines in both conception and production. The slender, courtly elegance of Italian or French Mannerism was not entirely to the German taste.

The workshops continued their local production of the monuments or religious icons for such areas as remained Catholic.

Only in the smaller works in ivory or boxwood (*Ill.* 226), or in the silverware and medals, does something of a great tradition remain. Even in the Catholic areas Puritan influences were strong, and neither in quantity nor quality was the sculpture comparable to what had gone before. Besides the monuments, ornamental architectural features such as doors or fireplaces continued to provide sculptors with an outlet, though here again the work was often of rather indifferent quality. The sixteenth century Northern style which had developed in the Low Countries was predominant. Generally these works consist of lumpy figures or three-dimensional picture reliefs set into elaborate and —by our standards—rather heavy architectural frames. As in the Low Countries, this was a logical development from the Late Gothic workshops.

226 (*left*) Leonhard Kern: *Diana*. Boxwood, 9 in. high, mid seventeenth century.
227 (*right*) Jörg Zurn: Detail of the Virgin Mary from a group of the Annunciation. Painted wood, early seventeenth century.

Where figure sculpture is employed in the reliefs the focus is upon the narrative, and the artistic interest, such as it is, is in the technical ingenuity of an ever-greater elaboration of the grouping and ornaments. There is no idea of a sculptural work of art with flowing line or composition as these would have been understood in Italy. Even the better family workshops, such as that of the Zurns (*Ill.* 227), mostly produced works of a coarseness or self-conscious heaviness that makes it hard to believe that they were but the second-generation heirs of the great carvers of the early sixteenth century, and the immediate forerunners of the Rococo movement in all its brilliance.

Even among the sepulchral monuments there is nothing to compare with the best French examples. The cruder demands of war, of petty dynastic pretensions and castle intrigues seem to have replaced cultivated patronage. Where individual sculptors in the Italian Mannerist tradition stand out it is in the later sixteenth century, and then most of the leading artists, such as Hubert Gerhardt or Adrien de Vries or Johann Gregor v. der Schardt, were born in the Low Countries and studied in Italy under Giovanni Bologna, so that although they were vital to the stream of German art, and most of their lives were spent in the Germanic areas, they represent an exotic development. Nevertheless, some local talent stands out, as in the case of Jörg Petel (*Ill.* 228), a notable carver whether on a large scale or in smaller works in ivory and bronze. Hans Krumper (*Ill.* 229) and Hans Riechle are also deserving of mention, but even these artists were Italian-trained, or had absorbed the Italian influence, as a comparison of figures on their fountain with those on the great fountain by Bartolommeo Ammanati (*Ill.* 168) shows. Apart from such fairly rare examples it is not until the end of the seventeenth century, which we shall come to in the following section, that German sculpture begins once again to take up the great heritage of late medieval times, and to develop once more into a school of really outstanding quality.

228 Jörg Petel: *Venus and Cupid*. Ivory, 16 in. high, seventeenth century. The group is believed to have belonged to the painter Rubens, and then to the celebrated George Villiers, Duke of Buckingham.

229 Hans Krumper: *Justice*. Bronze, over life-size. Residenz, Munich. Early seventeenth century.

We have already noted the decline of English sculpture after Mid-Gothic times, and it is really not until well into the eighteenth century that there is a return to quality in the production of native artists. English sculpture of the sixteenth and early seventeenth centuries rarely rises above decorative carving, and stylistically is perhaps best regarded as a provincial extension of the Low Countries, whence most of the leading sculptors came. Not that the tombs, doorways and chimney-pieces which were the principal outlets during Elizabethan and Jacobean times are altogether lacking in charm, but even at their best they delight us more by their evocation of history and nostalgic reminders of village churches than by their aesthetic merits, such as can be claimed for the better sculptures of France and Italy, or even Spain.

Just as in the Low Countries and Germany, this type of production was dominated by the traditional family workshops, operating in the main provincial centres or, in the case of the best artists, in London. The distances involved were relatively small, and it was not impossibly expensive, at least for those who could aspire to the best, to commission sculpture in London, thereby helping to build up London's position as a sculptural centre as well as the focal point of the court and Society.

In recent years, praiseworthy research, mainly by a small group of amateurs, has brought to light a host of names, but unhappily even if this makes the study more interesting it does not improve the objects themselves. Artists such as the Hollemans, the Colts, and the Cures, all families from the Low Countries, were among the most outstanding practitioners, and certainly obtained most of the important commissions. Their Italo-Flemish style, with its architectural or bedstead-like sarcophagi, with or without testers and with kneeling or recumbent effigies and occasionally additional figures of virtues or children, is to be found throughout the land (*Ill.* 231). Occasionally a more up-to-

230 Nicholas Stone: Monument to the poet John Donne, St Paul's Cathedral, London. Marble, second quarter of the seventeenth century.

231 Monument to Sir John St John, his first and second wife and his children. Lydiard Tregoze, Wiltshire, England. Sixteenth to seventeenth century.

date tribute is paid to Italian fashion in the busts set in niches and architectural wall monuments, a somewhat stolid pastiche of Rome. This style seems to have been more often adopted by English-born sculptors than by the Flemings, and of these English artists Epiphanius Evesham, the Christmas family and the Marshalls may be mentioned.

It is not until we come to Nicholas Stone (1586-1647) that something approaching real sculptural quality returns. Stone was trained by his father-in-law, Hendrik de Keyser; his monument to the great poet John Donne in St Paul's Cathedral (*Ill.* 230) shows imagination and vivacity in handling of the overall composition, even if it does not match his subject's verse in penetrating analysis.

Attempting to pattern his court in England on those of Italy, Charles I patronized Bernini and encouraged Italian and French artists to settle in England. The Genoese bronze sculptor Francesco Fanelli and the Frenchman Hubert Lesueur did indeed settle in England, but their rather tame productions made little impression outside the immediate court circle, and it was not until after the Commonwealth in 1660 that English artists and patrons looked seriously to the Continent again.

SPAIN

Just as the Italian Renaissance has been treated as a development apart, so the Spanish sculpture of the sixteenth to eighteenth centuries may be seen as a separate, homogeneous manifestation somewhat outside the stream of the rest of Europe.

As we have seen, for Romanesque the northern Christian part of Spain was in the vanguard of the international development. But by Gothic times—except where Romanesque traditions persisted—such work as appears in Spain or the rest of the Iberian peninsula was no more than a provincial version of the current international French style (*Ill.* 232). If there were any particularly Spanish characteristics they may be held to be a certain solidity of the figures and their rather bulbous long-slit eyes. As Gothic progressed the Flemish influence became paramount in Spain as in England. Flemish models and Flemish artists created a school whose works would scarcely be questioned had they appeared in the Low Countries. By the sixteenth century, again as in England, Italian artists had exerted their influence.

Throughout the century the influence of the two sources of inspiration can readily be followed side by side. Pietro Torrigiano exercised considerable influence in the earlier part of the century, but perhaps the most impressive of the Italian works were those done for the court at the mid-century by Pompeo Leoni (*Ill. 233*).

232 (*left*) Siloe Workshop: Monument to Don Garcia Osorio, formerly in the church of San Pedro de Ocana, near Aranjuez, Spain. Marble, early sixteenth century.
233 (*right*) Pompeo Leoni: *Philip II*, Bronze, mid sixteenth century.

By the middle of the century a blending with native talent begins to appear in groups such as the great sculptured figures by Gregorio Fernández at Valladolid or those of Juan de Juní (*Ill.* 234). Whether the latter was of foreign origin as it has been claimed is of small importance, for both these sculptors—and others too—displayed a naturalism combined with theatre in their painted wood carvings that was entirely Spanish in sentiment, and that heralded the great new development away from provincial pastiches of foreign models.

That a truly Spanish school should start at this time is not surprising, since it coincides with the first real emergence of Spain as a political entity. It was only at the end of the fifteenth century, in the 1490s, that the famous Catholic sovereigns had united the kingdoms of Castile and Leon and finally driven the Moors from the south. The kingdom became a flourishing one, and eventually, when it passed to the Hapsburg administration under Charles V, the greatest empire in Europe.

For a time the most important commissions still went either to the older Flemish-influenced Gothic workshops like those of the Siloe (*Ill.* 232) or Millan, or to Italians like Leoni. But this

234 Juan de Juní: *The Entombment.* Painted wood, late sixteenth century.

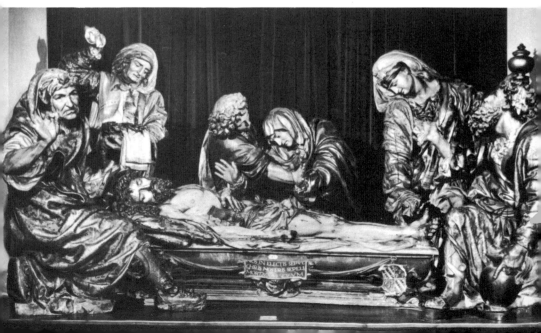

was soon to change. In the religious struggles then raging Spain had embraced her fidelity to the Catholic faith more violently perhaps than any other country. From the Crown to the meanest peasant the mainspring of every action—even to the colonial conquest of America—was Catholic Christianity. Spain became a focus of the struggle against heresy—even more perhaps than papal Rome. It was as the expression of this religious movement that the new sculpture of Spain evolved, and in turn it contributed to it. Above all, sculpture adopted the main theme of the Counter-Reformation, led by the Spanish saint Ignatius Loyola, which was that the individual should try to identify himself with the sufferings of holy persons, the saints and martyrs, and our Lord and his mother particularly at the Passion.

In such representations, emphasis on exact rendering of detail inherited from the Flemish northern influences blended with a Mediterranean emotional humanism and the Italian example. These ingredients were obviously likely to create a powerful theatrical illusionistic art, and this is indeed manifest in the sculpture that developed. By the end of the sixteenth century and during the seventeenth there grew up a school of carvers whose influence has never really died out. Particularly in the south this is Counter-Reformation sculpture *par excellence.*

Since the purpose of this art was the life-like representation of human beings (usually at a moment of intense suffering) it is often extremely difficult to distinguish between one artist and another. Even acknowledged experts tend to change their minds about attributions, or to hesitate among the great wood carvers such as Martínez Montañéz, Pedro de Mena or José de Mora —whose workshops were in any case as extensive as those in Gothic Germany. If there is any stylistic independence it is rather in choice of model than in technique and presentation. Thus Montañéz might choose a subject with the broader type of face that he admired while Mena seemed to prefer more intense, hatchet-faced models (*Ill. 235*). But in any of their sculptures

227

235 (*left*) Pedro de Mena: *Mary Magdalene*. Painted wood, life-size, seventeenth century.

236 (*right*) Pedro de Mena: *A Boy Saint*. Painted wood, life-size, seventeenth century.

the realism is so pronounced that there is little scope for individual artistic developments.

In this movement we can trace the effect of the Italian artists of the sixteenth century, who were influenced in their turn by the Spanish atmosphere; and at the same time, without the precise observation of the Flemish sources neither the veins on the hands nor the tears on the faces nor the blood on the flagellated bodies would have reached their extreme of detailed actuality. It is curious that even the great painters of the time—for this is also the great period of Spanish painting—did not develop quite the cinematic qualities of the sculptures. This school of sculpture established in the sixteenth century has continued right up to the present day almost unchanged.

In the mid seventeenth century it is chiefly represented by Alonso Cano, who worked as an architect, painter and sculptor, and was perhaps most successful in the latter role. At this time increasing use was made of materials such as real hair, lace and silks, so that some figures were merely heads and hands attached to a dummy. Pedro Roldán and his daughter Luisa Roldán worked in this style; the latter was responsible for the *Virgin of the Macerena* (*Ill.* 238), the famous bullfighter's icon, which it would be hard to surpass for the fantasy of its diamond tears, its lace and jewellery. In the eighteenth century there is sometimes a slight fussing of the drapery when it was carved, as in the case of an artist like Rixueno, but in both Spain and Portugal the style as a whole alters little between the seventeenth and

237 Pedro de Mena:
The Virgin of Sorrows.
Painted wood, life-size,
seventeenth century.

238 Luisa Roldán: *The Virgin of the Macerena*, Seville. Painted wood, precious stones and fabrics. Late seventeenth century.

twentieth centuries, as the work of an artist like Sarcillo shows.

Prejudice against this movement of intense religious illusionism is heightened by the Technicolor in which it is conceived. This Spanish sculpture looks like, and was intended to provide exactly the same emotional stimulus as the Hollywood tear-jerkers at the height of the emotional period of the 'twenties. The Spaniards had the advantage of being able to use colour, and this, together with the real lace, gold, pearls and jewellery that they had not the slightest hesitation about piling on, created an art for the people, which has not only continued in favour in Spain right up to the present time, but, we would suspect, contributed more strongly to the plaster Catholic sculptures today than almost any other source—even the paintings of Carlo Dolci or Sassoferrato. It is essentially a popular art, and if we accept its own statement, or even Reynolds' comment that 'the excellence of every art depends on the complete achievement of its purpose', this is an art that surely deserves to be called excellent.

230

The Mid Seventeenth to Eighteenth Centuries

A little more than one hundred years after the great political changes of the second quarter of the sixteenth century a new series of events, which had considerable effect on the arts, spread through most of the Northern countries. The most important of these events, if not chronologically the first, was Louis XIV's final triumph as an absolute monarch, followed by the visible expression of his power in the building of the palace of Versailles. The decorations of this palace were all important as an influence on sculpture in Northern Europe, and the French style spread all over Europe as other princes sought to emulate the superb achievement according to their means or imagination.

Elsewhere, the end of the Thirty Years' War in 1648 had brought about some respite and sense of security within the various areas of Germany and the Empire. It ushered in a period when the arts, especially in the Catholic south, could begin to flourish once again. In the Low Countries the *status quo* was ratified by recognition of the independence of the Protestant states of Holland, and this, by dividing more clearly the non-Catholic and Catholic areas, had helped to advance the progress of sculpture in the latter. In England the Restoration of the Monarchy in 1660 was followed by an extended period of internal peace—the first for several centuries. The social and economic advances that followed on these events in the various countries set the stage once more for a notable revival of European sculpture in the eighteenth century.

The stylistic streams remained fundamentally as before, with the division between the sensual and the disciplined, the Aristotelian and the Platonic. But the cleavage is perhaps slightly less marked than in earlier centuries, and at the beginning of the period most countries inclined towards the rather heavily sensuous of the Counter-Reformation and Baroque. As the eighteenth century went on, however, apart from areas of German Rococo, a formal classicism takes an increasing hold, culminating in the almost Puritan neo-classical mood of the period round 1800.

In all this there is some decrease of emphasis in the division between the Mediterranean and the North, due to the fact that while Italy generally and Rome in particular were still the training-ground for artists and dilettantes alike, Rome itself became profoundly influenced by the foreigners there, especially the French. The combination of these influences led to the evolution of a fairly international style, in which the intellectual romanticism of the subject matter was intimately bound up with current philosophies and intellectual tenets, and tempered by the eighteenth century's interpretation of classical ideas.

Most important among these eighteenth-century modifications is perhaps the wearing thin of the classical ideals of detachment and chasteness in regard to the human body, and the introduction of an element of deliberate sex appeal by the sculptors. We have noted that Bernini's *Saint Theresa* is not only presented in very worldly terms but also accorded a physical allure the Saint cannot have possessed in real life. Although the Saint was still within living memory when this figure was carved, the licence of the artistic translation was regarded as quite proper. Spiritual beauty had to be associated with corporeal beauty.

By the eighteenth century this aspect had developed apace, as much for religious as for lay models, so that quite apart from the deliberately sensual pieces of a Clodion or Marin, many Rococo saints and martyrs, from Spain to Germany, are presented as desirable individuals fully conscious of their charms. For so exquisite a society the unwashed reality of sanctity might have been as inconvenient as over-insistence on spiritual virtues.

232

The current philosophical and intellectual attitudes to art, which had been very important both to painting and sculpture ever since the Renaissance, took on a new significance with the constitution and increasing control of the new national academies. Since the authorities who controlled these institutions also virtually controlled all places, commissions and pensions, any theories held by them were likely to be extremely influential. They in turn were likely to be strongly affected by the opinions of the courts, or of the writers, philosophers and intellectuals of the salons. So it was that Descartes profoundly influenced Lebrun and thereby the whole Versailles development. Later the salons played a large part in moulding the period's taste. In the same way the work of archaeologists and scholars like Winckelmann lay at the root of the neo-classical movement.

The classical interpretations were further influenced, as far as the academies were concerned, by the increasing interest in scientific research, which for sculpture included not only anatomy but what is now termed psychology as well. F.X Messerschmidt, for example, was a friend of Mesmer, and his series of more than sixty heads, representative of the human passions, was almost clinical in its observation (*Ill.* 256). In this he differed from the ordinary artist only in intensity, not in type of approach.

Academic dominance made for a control that was nearly as rigid as the iconography of the early Church. Independent activity was not encouraged. With the possible exception of Rococo in Germany, a strict conformity with etiquette was expected of artists in both the selection of subject matter and in expression.

It must not be held that the authorities intended to be illiberal. In imposing conventions and rules they intended only to assist in the creation of works of art, and the quality of a work of art in its own right, as accepted at the Renaissance, was well appreciated. At least one result of all this academic training was that sculpture throughout Europe reached a very high standard of technical excellence. Even artists of the second rank were often highly-skilled executants. Indeed a balanced appreciation of this wide range of high quality work is made difficult by its sheer quantity. A corollary to this arises towards the later half of the century, when sculptors were often so overwhelmed by their technical interests that content was eclipsed by virtuosity, as in France with artists like Marin, or with the Neapolitans.

These classical influences affected not only the lay sculptures which proliferated on monuments and fountains, in gardens and houses, but also the religious works of the period. Madonnas and saints still appeared as classical worthies in elaborate drapery, posed like any Roman orator, as they had under Baroque. But in the eighteenth century a greater conformity of gesture and emphasis on personal attraction replaced the violence of earlier periods.

In contrast to this general conformity was the stupendous flowering of South German Rococo, in which for once the North led a revolt against classical disciplines.

The small sculptures, *Kleinplastik*, continued to flourish, and from the seventeenth century onwards discerning *cognoscenti* were also anxious to collect sketches for sculpture, often in terracotta, in the same way as they collected preliminary drawings for paintings. In porcelain the modellers found an entirely new field of activity.

FRANCE

The promotion of the Sun King and the progress of Versailles, which had so profound an effect on life and the arts in France, at first brought about an increase in the quantity of sculpture, rather than any fundamental change in the Italian-classical tradition which had persisted since the time of Fontainebleau.

Of course some concession was made to Baroque in the elaboration of composition and movement, but the French disciplines are very evident. Commemorative statues still persisted, though the great impetus of Versailles was towards decorative, and especially garden sculpture, which proliferated once the building approached completion. Interesting evidence of this

239 Antoine Coysevox: *Mercury*. Gardens of the Tuileries, France. Marble, late seventeenth century.

is an account for Versailles dating from 1692, which lists some fifty artists working on groups, figures or vases for the gardens alone. Only a handful of these artists are at all well known today, among them Coysevox (*Ill.* 239), Desjardins, Girardon, Lefebeure, Lehongre, Slodz, Tuby and Van Cleve. The sums they each received do not appear to differ a great deal, which suggests that at the time they were all held in more or less similar regard.

In all these works classical-allegorical themes predominate, whether in groups (*Ill.* 240) or in single figures or reliefs. While the subjects and their treatment may seem strange today, at the time their moral—or for that matter immoral—significance was common knowledge in the exclusive society for which they were created. The same subjects that served for sculpture frequently served for painting and the theatre too.

Besides these decorative works there was an enthusiastic acceptance of the Baroque period's delight in portraiture (*Ill.* 241). Artists like Coustou and Lemoyne joined with some of those

240 Gaspard and Balthasar Marsy: The Fountain of Latona in the Gardens of the Palace of Versailles. Marble, c. 1670.

who had worked on the Versailles garden sculpture to lay the foundations of a notable development, which was to spread widely in the following century.

Most important of all for sculpture was the extension of court patronage. From this time onwards until the Revolution the court dominated the arts in France. It attracted all the established artists as well as protecting the apprentices. Everyone sought and many found employment there, unless it happened that they were personally or stylistically uncongenial. Puget's Baroque tendencies, for instance, at first found no favour.

The great Bernini himself was summoned to Paris, where he executed portraits of Louis XIV and designed a new palace for the Louvre. Yet he was quickly set aside, no doubt partly because of intrigues, but also because his ebullience was fundamentally distasteful. A community which idolized Racine was unlikely to take very readily to the freedoms of Baroque.

236

Though as later no illiberality was intended, this almost total domination by court circles meant that the accepted academic traditions were the rule. In Paris itself, and at the Academy of France in Rome, whither went most successful students to study for a period of years as direct pensioners of the King, the control and supervision were strict, and an almost blind acceptance of the measured classical traditions prevailed. An interesting consequence of this situation is the return of something akin to the Gothic workshop tradition. It is often difficult to make ascriptions on purely stylistic grounds, since not only was there an easy interchangeability of the sculptors working on any piece or project, but also, as in Gothic times, the overall design and even detailed planning of these vast operations had to be undertaken by a director. Thus at Versailles it might be Lebrun or Mignard, who were painters, rather than Girardon, the leading sculptor, who directed the work and even designed details for the groups of figures. Although lip-service and even adulation was accorded to individual artists, all the circumstances made any deviation from accepted formulae as difficult as would have been departure from strict social etiquette for an aristocrat. It is noteworthy

241 Antoine Coysevox: Bust of the Painter Lebrun. Terracotta, late seventeenth century.

237

that again almost all the sculptors belonged, as in Flanders or Germany, to artist families, often several generations old.

In this hieratic social organization the academies were not the only important influence on sculpture. There were the King's mistresses, and informed or uninformed aristocrats of proud enough lineage, who joined with intellectuals, members of salons and clubs, philosophers and writers to make their impact. This had been the case at all periods since the Renaissance, to a greater or lesser degree, and the influence was by no means necessarily bad. We emphasize it here merely because in eighteenth-century France it became especially penetrating. For good or ill, the artificialities of etiquette, as we may regard them, which dominated the court, dictated the sculpture. The results were charming, delightful, civilized works, of no greater penetration than the strict etiquettes of this particularly refined society would allow. As an illustration of the conventions in action we have the story, from the later period, of Bouchardon's statue of *Love cutting his Bow from the Club of Hercules (Ill. 242)*. After a number of years, and having been adjudged of some aesthetic merit, this piece was finally received at court. But when it was exposed at Versailles the ladies tittered that they could not understand why Love should be represented as concerned with

242 Edmé Bouchardon: *Love cutting his Bow from the Club of Hercules*. Marble, eighteenth century.

238

clubs. The witty critic Diderot commented on the same lines. Even Voltaire was critical—not of any aesthetic demerits of the object, but because he could not see that a god should be allowed to do manual work. In the end this charming figure was relegated to the Orangery at Choisy, a revealing indication of how the court viewed sculpture, and the influence it could exert.

The technical influences still came chiefly from Italy, and especially, now, through the French Academy at Rome, first promoted some time earlier, but finally established in 1661. Students normally spent some years there in academic study of the ancients, paying a certain amount of attention—but not too much—to all the past and current Italian masterpieces. The combination created the new style. The importance of this Academy was not limited to France: the Gallic influence on Italian sculpture through exponents like Monnot or Legros was profoundly significant.

The Academy also furnished copies or casts of ancient marbles for the French capital. While sometimes these were in bronze, on other occasions the plasters were sent for casting in France and in the process, modifications or restorations might be made, as the accounts bear witness. The perfectionists of Versailles did not approve of mutilated fragments, but they saw no objection to taking some classical piece and adapting it as a garden statue.

But sculpture in France was not entirely limited to decorative work for palaces and monuments to the King. Despite the destruction which took place at the Revolution, the churches throughout the country bear witness to an increase in religious carving. In this work the stylistic influences appear generally to have been fairly traditional. Once again it is often difficult to decide, not only between ascription to one artist or another, but even, on occasion, whether the piece belongs to the seventeenth, eighteenth, or even sixteenth century, for the styles introduced by Goujon and Pilon persisted over a long period. And once again monuments and tombs play an important part in sculpture.

239

While the overall style evolved in the second half of the seventeenth century persisted more strongly in sculpture than in painting or furniture, the advent of Louis XV brought about a change. The mid-century sculptors show a greater sensuality and lightness. Although most leaders were trained in Rome and in some cases—L.S. Adam and Falconet, for instance—were known admirers of Bernini, they show little of the bravura of Baroque, as indeed little of the gaiety and fantasy even of contemporary German Rococo. To controlling influences such as the academies and salons, the exuberance of the one was as distasteful as the indiscipline of the other. Indeed, although the Rococo movement took its inspiration primarily from France and flourished in the minor arts, it was never to make any great headway in French sculpture. Whatever the court morals may have been, court manners seem to have eschewed anything that smacked of indecorum in its sculpture, which remained rather formal under the tutelage of the established academies of Paris and Rome. It is

243 (left) J. H. Fragonard: Detail of a panel painting entitled *The Meeting*. The Frick Collection, New York. Eighteenth century.

244 (right) Etienne Falconet: *Bathing Girl*. Marble, eighteenth century.

245 (*left*) Claude Michel, called Clodion: *Cupid and Psyche*. Terracotta, 23½ in. high. Late eighteenth century.

246 (*right*) J. A. Houdon: *Madame Victoire*. Portrait bust, eighteenth century.

perhaps significant that when he painted a statue for the exquisite series of panels in the Frick Collection, Fragonard chose a model far more akin to Ignaz Günther than any sculpture that ever came out of France (*Ill.* 243, cf. 250).

As in the case of the seventeenth-century artists, the sculptors of the mid-eighteenth century are so numerous that it becomes almost invidious to mention names, so that although J. B. Lemoyne, Bouchardon, Pigalle, L. S. Adam, Falconet (*Ill.* 244) and Pajou stand out among the first generation of artists born in the eighteenth century and active under Louis XV, there were hundreds more.

Among the later generation we can point to Claude Michel, called Clodion (*Ill.* 245), a notable sculptor in the neo-classical

241

tradition, who together with artists like Marin and Boizot served the decorative needs of the reign of Louis XVI. The development of intimate, smaller works and sketches in terracotta, designed for the elegant and sophisticated rooms of the day, was an important feature with these artists, while in their more formal work they contributed to the particular form of neoclassicism which found favour in France.

Towards the end of the century it is Jean Antoine Houdon (1741-1829) whose work carries on the great traditions of French sculpture, whether in objects like the famous *Diana* or the splendid series of portrait busts (*Ill.* 246), which combine the best of the eighteenth century with some deference to the neoclassical trends elsewhere.

THE LOW COUNTRIES

In the seventeenth century political and religious differences had produced a sharp cleavage between the Flemish and the Dutch, and their inherent racial differences had led to widely divergent national schools of painting. Nevertheless sculpture seems to have remained predominantly a Flemish art, so that despite the political recognition of two separate entities, we may still be justified in regarding the Netherlands as a single unit for the purpose of the history of sculpture.

The factors that had brought about a revival of sculpture in Catholic Flanders at the start of the seventeenth century had also laid down the general line that the art was to follow for some time to come, so that there is less change in Flanders between 1600 and 1800 than elsewhere. Italian training was as much in demand as it had been in the sixteenth century, and the Roman-Italian classical style prevailed here also. The native translation of the Southern inspiration is akin to that of the French. It is a sharpening and a refinement of the Southern idiom rather than the exaggeration of the more Baroque characteristics that might have been expected from the homeland of Rubens.

Perhaps the most important aspect of Flemish sculpture at this period was, as in earlier periods, export—export now usually of artists rather than of works of art. The tradition of the Flemish guilds and family workshops still continued to produce artists of high technical competence, if not always of great originality or genius. As in the fifteenth and sixteenth centuries, so in the seventeenth and eighteenth these artists sought to emigrate. Northern sculpture would have been a very different affair without them, and many of the sculptors claimed by one nation or another prove to have been of Netherlandish stock.

France may claim Bogaert (Desjardins), Van Cleve, Opstal and many others; Willem de Groff with his work for the German courts, including the famous and enchanting *Silver Prince* (*Ill.* 247) really belongs to Germany, while England was dependent for much of her best work on her Flemish immigrants. The Quellins, Van Gelder, Scheemakers, Rysbrack, Delvaux, Nollekens, even Grinling Gibbons, and a score of others who worked in England for short periods or of life, were the mainstay of her sculpture for the first half of the eighteenth century.

247 Willem de Groff: *Crown Prince Maximilian von Bayern.* Silver, half life-size, mid eighteenth century. Made as a votive offering for the Prince's recovery from an illness.

248 Luc Faid'herbe: Monument to the Berthout family, Church of St Rombout, Malines. Marble, seventeenth century.

At the same time, not all the artists sought to emigrate. Notable among those who remained was Luc Faid'herbe (1617-1697) whose name was almost a byword, especially for small sculptures. The monument at Malines (*Ill.* 248) is witness to his sensitivity and potentialities on a larger scale. Gentler and more Gallic and painterly in approach than Duquesnoy, he may perhaps be taken as bringing in something of new tradition. Towards the end of the century a new generation of the Quellins, beginning with Artus II, provided works of distinction. Jean Delcour was another agreeable artist in the rather lyrical French tradition.

All these sculptors worked in a slightly modified version of the Franco-Italian style. The leading representative of the rather more robust tradition is perhaps Rombout Verhulst of Malines, not only a good sculptor but a particularly excellent portraitist, whose work is perhaps closer allied with Dutch than Flemish tradition. For all these sculptors the main outlet in Flanders was church sculpture or monuments. Some garden figures were produced, but on the whole, decorative sculptures were confined to minor artists.

Among the more interesting developments of these centuries was a local revival of wood sculpture on an elaborate scale, as in such astonishing pulpits as those of 1669 by Verbruggen at Brussels (*Ill.* 249), and those at Malines—one by Vervoort of 1721 and another by Theodor Verhaegen of 1743. These no

249 H. F. Verbruggen: *Adam and Eve banished from Paradise*. Detail from a pulpit, in the Cathedral of St Gudule, Brussels. Marble, seventeenth century.

doubt owe much to Southern German inspiration in their ingenuity and Rococo spirit, though they are considerably more
stolid. They also betoken the re-emergence of the old Netherlandish technical facility in wood.

This facility in wood-carving is expressed, too, in the *Kleinplastik*, which continued as before both in Flanders and in Holland. The work of the Xavery family of Holland is particularly
agreeable.

The elaborate foliage-carving of the late seventeenth century
is often so fine as to deserve mention under the heading of sculpture. It was used for furniture such as choir stalls or stands and
tables, and enjoyed popularity well outside the Low Countries.
The carving of Grinling Gibbons, who worked all his life in
England, was a masterly example.

At the end of the century Flanders followed on the French
trend of neo-classicism, rather than on the more formal schools
elsewhere. Of this style Godescharle is perhaps the most distinguished exponent.

GERMANY

The political event which brought so great a change to Germany
in the mid seventeenth century was the ending of the devastating
Thirty Years' War in 1648. As in England, peace brought about
no immediate artistic outburst, but circumstances began to improve all round, and by the later part of the century the ground
was prepared for the astonishing flowering of the South German
Rococo in the second decade of the eighteenth century.

Nearly all the outstanding achievements of this period come
from the south, or from artists trained in the south. This area
was virtually the same as that which had produced the great
sculptures of the early sixteenth century: Bavaria, Swabia and
Franconia, with a reflection from Vienna, capital of the Empire,
allied though not necessarily dependent. These were all Catholic
countries, and the full development of Rococo was most effecti-

246

250 Ignaz Günther: Group of Apostles, from the decoration of the Chapel of Schloss Sünching, near Regensburg. Painted wood, mid eighteenth century.

251 J. B. Neumann and others: The interior of the Church of Vierzehnheiligen, Bavaria.

vely directed to the rebuilding or redecoration of the churches. Lay sculptures usually conformed to a rather set style, with groups of the seasons, or figures designed for halls and stairways or gardens. They appear in profusion in the great palaces built for the leading princes in various parts of the land. Occasionally more modest private patrons went further than the merely decorative, as in the splendid Günther Chapel and rooms in Schloss Sünching (*Ill.* 250). Garden sculptures were popular, as in the notable group by Dietz from the gardens of Veithöchsheim, now in Würzburg. The inspiration for all this undoubtedly originated in Versailles, and the earlier undertakings were in the Grand Manner, but very soon the native elements asserted themselves and a purely German style was evolved by the local artists—destined to become one of the most astonishing combined operations of sculpture, painting, architecture and decoration that the world has ever seen.

At the start the movement was fairly general and widespread, following a wave of religious enthusiasm and revival in Catholic areas at the end of the seventeenth century. The first sculptures were still rather stodgy and provincially Baroque in character, though something of the new gaiety comes in with the Schluters at Berlin around 1700, or the superlative carvings by Permoser and others in Dresden during the next decade (*Ill.* 252), which are a landmark for quality even in the cultivated Saxon capital.

Soon after the turn of the century Rococo gathered momentum, especially at the end of the War of the Austrian Succession in 1711. Then came a spate of building and rebuilding all over the southern territories, particularly in the churches, which became ever lighter, more theatrical and gay, culminating in such triumphs as Vierzehnheiligen (*Ill.* 251) or Die Wies. In these the style loosened with the most perfect harmony of fantasy that the carefully co-ordinated activity of sculptors, painters, architects and stucco workers could achieve. Frivolous and theatrical though such creations may sometimes seem—and it is for this

252 Balthasar Permoser: Supporting figures from the entrance to the Zwinger Gallery, Dresden. Stone, early eighteenth century.

that they have been condemned till very recently—it would be a mistake to think that the whole was not conceived and executed in a spirit of the deepest piety. The Asam brothers, for example, built their own chapel at their own expense.

While Rococo was essentially a popular expression of faith it came at a time when life, at least for the rich, had taken on something of the quality of the fairy tales handed down to us by the brothers Grimm. What better setting could there be for fairy princes and princesses than the *putti* and angels and fantasy of the South German Rococo? In this movement everyone could participate—and indeed, occasionally all did so practically, by voluntary labour on the building. Curiously enough this superlatively creative movement was made possible directly by tradition and owes almost everything to the family workshops which had managed to continue, either at the princely capitals or in the great mercantile centres such as Augsburg or Nuremberg, ever since late Gothic times. The talent which had flowered so effectively in 1500 had faded out in the next generation and revived from comparative dormancy towards 1700, when the old traditions re-adapted themselves to the new style. Whatever debt may have been owed to French or Italian influences at the outset, the culmination is purely German and has a gaiety which is not to be found elsewhere. There is a ruthless treatment of material to create any fantasy that is asked of it. The sculptures, which are largely in painted wood, as in 1500, seem almost to disregard the substance in which they are made.

A considerable number of accounts and records still exist from this period, so we are able to put names and dates to most of the major creations of the day, but while the main workshops show reasonably distinct differences of handling, within the groups we find the same uniformity and anonymity as had existed among the craftsmen in a workshop in Gothic times.

253 Ignaz Günther: Male Saint. Painted wood, over life-size. Rott-am-Inn, Bavaria. 1759-63.

254 Franz Josef Holzinger: Christ with supporting figures. Stucco group on the High Altar, Altenburg, Austria.

Another similarity with the Middle Ages is the vast scale of the new undertakings, and the fact that however beautiful the individual figures or groups or pieces, they were conceived originally as part of a vast theatrical whole, and should always be considered in that context. Again as in Gothic, they were usually dependent upon the use of colour and gilding, which was applied in the same traditional way as in the times of Riemenschneider or the Lainbergers (*Ill.* 84), though perhaps to an even more lavish extent. As far as names can be singled out in Rococo, that of Ignaz Günther (*Ills.* 250, 253) is possibly pre-eminent among the Bavarians, but he is certainly closely followed up by Dietz, Straub, the Jorhans, Feichtmayer, the Asam brothers, Paul Egell in the Rhineland and a host of others. So powerful was the movement that Rococo continued long after other countries had taken up the neo-classical revival. It was only right at the end of the eighteenth century and at the beginning of the nineteenth that any notable change took place in Germany.

Outside the south-western area the Viennese court was the largest as well as the richest centre of the Germanic territories, and here a school grew up whose chief exponent is Rafael Donner (*Ill. 255*). Donner and a group of other sculptors such as Hagenauer, Stammell or Balthazar Moll were responsible for most of the works in Austria, including the enormously elaborate and rather heavily loaded monuments of the Imperial family. These are achievements worthy of respect. Rather later in the century, F. X. Messerschmidt stands out for his famous series of busts portraying the human emotions (*Ill. 256*).

The later Berlin decorative sculptors working for Frederick the Great at Potsdam represent a rather isolated effort in this otherwise somewhat deserted area in Northern Germany.

Alongside the very large scale works, tombs and monuments went on, usually in a slightly more traditional vein, but far from inevitably so. *Kleinplastik*, which had persisted so happily right through from the sixteenth century, produced works of great

255 (*left*) G. R. Donner: *Providence*. Bronze, eighteenth century.
256 (*right*) F. X. Messerschmidt: *Character head*. Lead, mid eighteenth century.

elegance and refinement both in boxwood and ivory. Perhaps the most generally popular objects were the models created for the great new ceramic factories that had started up by the middle of the century all over the territory. If the name of Kaendler is outstanding at Dresden, there were also Weyer in Berlin, the family von Lücke, and many others of distinction.

ENGLAND

At last, in the eighteenth century, England once again began to produce a native school of sculpture with which she could be reasonably content—even proud—after the doldrums of half a millenium. It must be admitted that at least at the start many of the leading protagonists were of foreign stock; but some had settled in England for so long and had so identified themselves with the country that they may reasonably be described as English artists. These immigrants perhaps led the more advanced development, but even the traditional native workshops and craftsmen began to produce monuments and busts of a quality that far transcended the provincial mason's work hitherto general.

At the end of the seventeenth century and in the earlier part of the eighteenth, sculptors like the Stantons, Bushnell (*Ill. 258*), Bird and the Greens of Camberwell were working in a reasonably attractive if rather a traditional style, which could be regarded as rather outmoded, if judged by contemporary French or Italian standards. The tenor is often very English in its restraint. On monuments, for example, there is usually a hesitancy in the rhetoric of the pose of the deceased, and none of the insolent bravura to be seen in the full Continental productions. The handling, too, is quietly naturalistic, and this becomes a particular feature in the portrait busts, of which Edward Pierce was at this time one of the better exponents (as in his portrait of *Christopher Wren* in the Ashmolean Museum, Oxford, executed in 1673, *Ill.* 257).

As for the immigrants of the seventeenth century, such as the Nosts or Grinling Gibbons, some were little superior to the native

257 (*left*) Edward Pierce: *Sir Christopher Wren*. Marble, late seventeenth century.
258 (*right*) J. Bushnell: *Sir Thomas Gresham*. The Old Bailey, London. Stone, seventeenth century.

artists. Gibbons as a sculptor in stone, as opposed to a wood carver, leaves much to be desired. But between the foreign influence and the home development the first decade of the eighteenth century saw considerable advance. In the next generation the better home workshops improved considerably. With artists like Sir Robert Taylor and Sir Henry Cheere they represented the family workshop persistence and provided agreeable and workmanlike monuments, which, if not always of the delicacy of the best in Italy or France, yet had a certain quality.

This developing school received a fillip in the second and third quarters of the eighteenth century with several more influential artists from abroad, some of whom came for a short time like Laurent Delvaux (between 1717 and 1726) while others stayed virtually for life. The two most outstanding of these were Michael Rysbrack (1694-1770) and Louis François Roubiliac (1702-1762). Rysbrack came to England in his mid-twenties in about 1720, and by the next decade had established his position as a leading sculptor—especially for portrait busts and monuments for which he was well patronized (*Ill.* 260). Roubiliac, possibly a pupil of Permoser, came over in 1735. He was not very successful at first, but after he had created the Argyle monument in 1748 (*Ill.* 259) his reputation forged ahead. Both these artists worked in the international Franco-Italian style and produced works of more than ordinary quality, Roubiliac with a Rococo bias, Rysbrack more classically Flemish.

Other immigrants in the earlier part of the century included the Italian Antonio Guelfi, Van Gelder, the Scheemakers—a family of artists who remained in England—and many more

259 L. F. Roubiliac: Monument to the Duke of Argyle, Westminster Abbey, London. Marble, 1748.

whose names are less well remembered today. In the latter category towards the end of the eighteenth century there is Joseph Nollekens, a second-generation Flemish artist whose work was highly regarded in his own day, and deservedly so, as we see if we look at the charming figure he designed for the mausoleum at Brocklesby (*Ill.* 261).

But local talent was also well established by the middle of the century with artists like Joseph Wilton, R.A., a truly sensitive sculptor whether in his monuments or busts (*Ill.* 262). The elder Bacon (1740-1799) may reasonably be included in the same category (*Ill.* 263). Both Wilton and Bacon could compare with all but the best elsewhere.

With the Protestant bias everywhere the demand for religious sculpture was practically non-existent, and the emphasis was on the personal monument, which became increasingly elaborate

260 (*left*) J. M. Rysbrack: Monument to Sir John Dutton, Sherborne, Dorset. Marble, 1749.
261 (*right*) Joseph Nollekens: Life-size figure of the Countess of Yarborough, 1787. Mausoleum at Brocklesby Park, Lincolnshire. Marble, life-size.

262 (*left*) Joseph Wilton: *Oliver Cromwell,* Marble. Signed and dated 1762.

263 (*right*) John Bacon: Monument to Sir William Blackstone. All Soul's College, Oxford. Marble, 1784.

with the developing dynastic pretensions of the Whigs. In the same way the bust became almost a requisite for the richer and more cultivated homes. Here the rather hesitant, naturalistic English tradition of understatement tended to persist even among the immigrant sculptors. Where there was any deviation from straight portraiture it was chiefly confined to the arrangement of a toga, or to classical armour to set off the head. This convention resulted no doubt from the fashion prevailing among men of taste throughout the eighteenth century for collecting Roman sculptures.

Decorative work was rarely called for, apart from a few pastiche classical reliefs for Palladian halls. There were also a certain number of garden figures, though because of the English climate most of these were lead casts of classical or pseudo-classical models, with occasional exceptions such as the popular shepherds and shepherdesses from the foundries of Sir Henry Cheere. These last pay token tribute to the Rococo movement, of which another reflection in English sculpture was the developing porcelain manufacture, notably at Chelsea.

By the end of the century a neo-classical school had begun to grow up which could reasonably hold its own at this generally rather unfortunate juncture in European sculpture. If Flaxman's name is the best-known, he was not perhaps the finest exponent, and sculptors like the younger Bacon and Sir Richard Westmacott (*Ill.* 264) or Chantrey, who lived well into the nineteenth century, may today command greater respect as artists.

264 Sir Richard Westmacott: Negro from the monument to Charles James Fox in Westminster Abbey, London. Marble, 1810.

The Nineteenth Century

Although the neo-classical movement did not develop fully until the very end of the eighteenth century, the foundations had been laid some decades earlier when classical preoccupations and classical studies took a more serious archaeological turn.

As early as the middle of the century the English Society of Dilettanti had financed two artists to make drawings of the antiquities of Greece. The French quickly followed suit, and afterwards individuals such as St Non or the great architect-decorator Robert Adam undertook somewhat liberal surveys of their own. Excavations had begun at Pompeii and Herculaneum which made a great stir and caught the public fancy. All these studies were published with unending commentaries on classical life and literature, and scholars like Winckelmann commanded world-wide interest and respect. So the stage was set for a neo-classical revival in which classical life as a whole and the classical interpretations of sculpture became intriguing to everyone.

The revolutionary movements, which were by no means confined to France, adopted a noble Roman pose. Napoleonic neo-classicism was to take over these canons, not only in sculpture but in all the arts, including architecture, painting, and even furniture and women's clothes. A 'classic' simplicity became the order of the day. Earlier Greek examples, or Roman copies from them, rather than late Imperial Roman models became the ideal, though when Lord Elgin brought his marbles to England from Greece they aroused little greater general interest than the pastiches of contemporary sculptors.

This whole movement was designed to clear away what was then regarded as a rather make-believe classicism, which had gone on in one form or another since the Renaissance. By 1800 it was only rarely, as with the great French sculptor Houdon, that something of the eighteenth-century tradition persisted. Once it was really established by the opening of the nineteenth century, the new movement became truly European to a degree that had perhaps not been the case since Gothic, with Canova in Italy (*Ill.* 266), Flaxman in England, artists like Thorwaldsen in Denmark (*Ill.* 267) and Schadow in Germany (*Ill.* 268) all equally representative.

The sculpture of this pagan inspiration was not limited to busts or figures but included the sepulchral monuments which were still the chief outlet for carvers. In these monuments any recognizable Christian allusions usually moved to the epitaph, and became virtually secondary to the lay tributes of relicts mourning their toga-clad deceased among obelisks, sarcophagi and classical

265 (*left*) Joseph Nollekens: Monument to Sir Thomas and Lady Salusbury, Great Offley Church, Hertfordshire, England. Marble, 1777.

266 (*right*) Antonio Canova: *Theseus and the Minotaur*. Marble. Italian, 1782. Height 58¼ in.

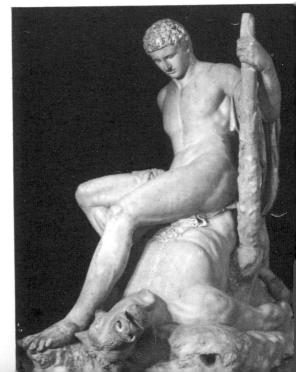

vases. We can observe the transition in Nollekens' Salusbury monument (*Ill. 265*), in which the noble Roman and his matronly lady still have some slight eighteenth-century humanity in their rendering. But by the turn of the century this had vanished.

Alongside the new classicizing came a passionate concern with exact naturalistic representation in every field of art. The attitude of mind behind all this is tellingly conveyed in a contemporary (1825) English biography of Canova by J. S. Memes: 'It was his [Canova's] frequent exercise to draw, or more generally to model, for several successive days, from the living subject. In thus diligently imitating, he never allowed his imagination in the slightest manner to deviate from nature, as presented to his view, on these occasions.' Subsequently even the writer felt constrained to add that such exercises 'possessed no more enlarged ideas of beauty than such as nature exhibits to the observer'.

267 (*left*) Barthel Thorwaldsen: *Shepherd-Boy*. Marble. Danish, early nineteenth century.

268 (*right*) Johann Gottfried Schadow: *The Princesses Luise and Frederika of Prussia*. Marble, 1795-7.

An art which was so very much an imitation, whether of nature or of another epoch, naturally discouraged individuality among artists, and this uniformity appeared as much in the work of those at the top as in that of the hundreds of their followers. They formed the taste in sculpture, and this taste was to continue in the academies and dominate the graveyards right through the nineteenth century. As illustration of its strong persistence it is perhaps sufficient to cite Gibson's *Tinted Venus* from the 1851 Exhibition (*Ill.* 269) or the famous Hiram Power's *Slave* in the United States.

This whole development, with its vast ramifications in the styles which came to join it in the rich nineteenth-century world has yet to be studied seriously. Before we can attempt even an outline we must stress the way in which the vast spread of wealth and with it the growth of a rich bourgeoisie expanded the outlet for sculpture and altered its tone. Henceforward it was no longer only the courts and aristocracy or cultivated amateurs who commissioned sculpture for their tombs or their homes. Almost every individual or public body with any pretension began to regard as a duty the promotion of sculpture if not its actual possession. By the second quarter of the nineteenth century it

269 John Gibson: *The 'Tinted Venus'.* Marble with slight pigmentation. English, *c.* 1850. Height 68 in.

270 Samuel Joseph: Seated figure from the monument to Wilberforce, Westminster Abbey, London. Marble, 1833.

was esteemed as a visible expression of cultivated status. Public monuments to kings, generals or great statesmen, to political events, wars or peace, abounded in the large cities, but in addition local mayors and worthies, doctors and artists, writers and benefactors were all recorded in marble or bronze until almost every village could boast one or more of such objects. The quantity of these has never been assessed, but the memories of travel anywhere in Europe are sufficient to make the most ardent corpus compiler quail. And if we add the innumerable carved graveyard figures the situation becomes even more unmanageable. In all these sculptures the demand was for an exact, photographic representation. The monument to Wilberforce in Westminster Abbey (*Ill.* 270) is an effective but typical example. To meet the demand schools and academies, both public and private, were founded and flourished, and it must be admitted that the technical competence of a great deal of the work is extremely high.

As the momentum increased and new monuments rose to right and left, the idea was extended to purely decorative sculptures in parks and squares, so that by the second quarter of the century vases and fountains, nymphs and animals vied for attention with the local dignitaries. With these works a new element of romantic lyricism came in to counter the classical severity, as when Rude created his Romantic revivals as early as the 1830s. Thereafter both schools existed side by side and there was money enough for both.

This Romantic movement laid the foundations of the lyrical, naturalistic style with Baroque overtones which continued through Rodin and in the academies well into the twentieth century. Elements of the style are present even in artists like Epstein.

A perspective of the movement has still not been seriously drawn up. For the ordinary person the problem is the difficulty of gaining access to this great range of sculpture. The case is not like that of literature or music, or even painting, which can be reproduced and presented from decade to decade with comparative ease. The expense of fine photography and reproduction is such that publications on sculpture cannot be made unless

271 François Rude: Monument designed as *The Imperial Eagle watching over Napoleon*. Bronze, *c.* 1845.

272 (*left*) J. B. Carpeaux: *Dancer with Tambourine*. A version of the popular bronze which appears in so many variations and sizes. French, approximately 20 in. high.

273 (*right*) Jules Dalou: *A Woman Reading*. Terracotta sketch model,
French, 9 in. high, *c.* 1875.

there is wide demand, and without publication the demand is
less likely to arise. It is a familiar impasse.

As a consequence, the mass of sculptors contemporary with
Verdi or Wagner, Dumas or Trollope, Turner, Menzel or Cézanne
are as yet, by comparison, unsifted, and unknown to this generation. Apart perhaps from Rodin, the movement is today generally only at all familiar through the work of its last heirs and
successors among the older living academicians, rather than from
the period at its full vigour.

The utilitarian aspect of so much of the best work, as an integral part of architecture, or as war memorials or personal portraits which are out of current fashion, may in itself inhibit our appreciation. How many Englishmen, for example, have ever studied the Albert Memorial as an outdoor museum of contemporary sculpture, which is what it was.

In addition to this more serious work came a mass of decorative sculpture, often produced on a commercial or semi-commercial scale. Here just as in literature or architecture or furnishing, designs from every field of previous inspiration were drawn upon. To join the respectable classical nude, usually now with fig leaf, came Teutonic knights or seventeenth-century gallants, pastiche Watteau shepherds or romantic Turks and Arabs. If there was little originality there was no end to the plagiarism.

274 (*left*) Alfred Stevens: *Virtue overcoming Vice*. Heroic-size plaster study for the Wellington Monument in St Paul's Cathedral, London. Third quarter of the nineteenth century.

275 (*right*) Vincenzo Gemito: *The Fisherboy*. Bronze, Italian, *c.* 1880.

276 Auguste Rodin: *The Muse*. Bronze, 57 in. high, *c.* 1896.

If any centre had the lead it was perhaps the schools of Paris, but in every country the output was so enormous that it would be difficult to point to any single source. If artists like Rude (*Ill.* 271), Carpeaux (*Ill.* 272), or later Dalou (*Ill.* 273) or Carrier Belleuse show one facet of the French school, culminating with Rodin (*Ill.* 276), England, with artists like Leighton, and especially Alfred Stevens (*Ill.* 274), Germany and indeed everywhere else showed others. In Italy the rich tourists who came with the new trains provided a gold mine. The catalogue of Neapolitan sculptors of the century alone runs into hundreds of pages of tiny print. The famous *Fisherboy* by Gemito (*Ill.* 275) is merely one of the better known of thousands of works in which the sugary and sensual prevailed. With these came hosts of sentimental angels for the tombs, or children, half Renaissance and half gutter, for the mantelpiece as well as the undertaker's yard. As if all this were not sufficient, the Catholic demand for saints and Virgins, at home or in missions abroad, was swelled by the new Protestant High Church movement.

Industrial development very quickly rose to meet all these tastes, and cheap metal or plaster casts were distributed for domestic consumption on a scale hitherto unprecedented. Multiple production served equally for dogs and cats, horses and birds, nudes and half-nudes, Negroes, Arabs, Indians, Chinese; for sculpture on furniture, sculpture on façades, sculpture on candlesticks, sculpture on clocks. There was no end to it in the halls or in the gardens, on the tables, on the mantelpieces, on the floors and on the ceilings.

Until today the styles have been too near us, so that besides the overwhelming quantity, a lack of sympathy has prevented any profitable assessment. After nearly a century, the time is ripe for the serious study of such works, but it will require a great deal of field-work and detachment before we can obtain a balanced perspective of this world-wide movement.

268

Select Bibliography

I Medieval Sculpture in the North

FRANCE

KINGSLEY PORTER, A. *Romanesque Sculpture of the Pilgrimage Roads,* Boston, 1923, 10 vols. Richly illustrates French Romanesque as well as Spanish.

The splendidly illustrated volumes of *Nuits des Temps* cover the various provinces.

GARDNER, A. *Medieval Sculpture in France, Cambridge,* 1931, affords an excellent groundwork.

AUBERT, M. *La Sculpture Française au Moyen Age,* Paris, 1946, and other recent editions of M. Aubert's work, are valuable and generally available, as is also:

VITRY, P. *French Sculpture during the Reign of St Louis 1226-1270,* Paris, 1931.

The illustrated catalogues of the Musée de Sculpture Comparée, though published some years ago, afford a valuable review.

An insight into the workings of the minds and masters of the Gothic period is provided by the following:

Abbé Suger on the Abbey Church of St Denis, translated by Erwin Panofsky, Princeton, 1946.

HAHNLOSER, H. R. *Villard de Honnecourt,* Vienna, 1935, among other facsimiles of the Album of Villard de Honnecourt.

GIMPEL, J. *Les Bâtisseurs de Cathédrals...,* Bourges, 1958.

The Late Gothic and Renaissance sculptors have been less conveniently treated, but:

KOECHLIN, R. *La Sculpture à Troyes...,* Paris, 1900, is a valuable study. And

BLUNT, A. *Art and Architecture in France, 1500 - 1700,* Harmondsworth, 1953, covers the 16th century from the Renaissance point of view.

Individual artists are treated in:

DAVID, H. *Claus Sluter,* Paris, 1951.

DAVID, H. *De Sluter à Sambin,* 2 vols, 1933.

PRADEL, P. *Michel Colombe, Le dernier imagier gothique,* Paris, 1953.

GERMANY

FEULNER, A. and MÜLLER, J. H. *Geschichte der deutschen Plastitk,* Munich, 1953, is a general survey.

German Romanesque is less widely significant than French, and has received less attention, but good reviews are to be found in the following:

BEENKEN, H. *Romanische Skulptur in Deutschland,* Leipzig, 1924.

GANTNER, J. *Romanische Plastik - Inhalt und Form in der Kunst des 11. und 12. Jahrhunderts,* Vienna, 1948.

In contrast, the literature on German Gothic is extremely rich. General works are:

STEINGRÄBER, E. *Deutsche Plastik der Frühzeit,* Königstein im Taunus, 1961.

REITZENSTEIN, A. F. von *Deutsche Plastik der Früh- und Hochgotik,* Königstein im Taunus, 1962.

SCHÄDLER, A. *Deutsche Plastik der Spätgotik,* Königstein im Taunus, 1962.

All in the Blauen Bücher series, and

WILM, H. *Die gotische Holzfigur,* 4th edition, Stuttgart, 1944.

Notable contributions have been made by such scholars as:

HALM, P.M. *Erasmus Grasser,* Augsburg, 1928.

MÜLLER, C.T. *Hans Leinberger,* Berlin, n.d.

SWOBODA, K. M. *Peter Parler,* Vienna, 1940.

FISCHEL, L. *Nicolaus Gerhaert und die Bildhauer der deutschen Spätgotik,* Munich, 1944.

PAATZ, W. *Bernt Notke und sein Kreis,* 2 vols, Berlin, 1939.

BIER, J. *Tilman Riemenschneider — die Frühen Werke,* Wurzburg, 1925, and the same—*Reifen Werke,* Augsburg, 1930.

DETTLOFF, S. *Wit Stosz,* 2 vols., Warsaw, 1961.

In addition most of the great cathedrals and abbey complexes have been fully treated from their special standpoint.

The volumes of the catalogues of Berlin Nuremberg, and Munich are basic for this time, and definitive for 16th century medals is:

HABICH, G. *Die deutschen Schaumünzen des XVI. Jahrhunderts,* Munich, 1929-34.

The 16th century is comprehensively reviewed in:

FEULNER, A. *Die deutsche Plastik des 16. Jahrhunderts,* Florence, Munich, 1926.

MÜLLER, T. H. *Deutsche Plastik der Renaissance,* Königstein im Taunus, 1963, in the Blauen Bücher series.

The increasingly important role of the *Kleinplastik* in the 16th century is covered by:

BANGE, E. F. *Die Kleinplastik der deutschen Renaissance,* Florence, Munich, 1928.

BANGE, E.F. *Die deutschen Bronzestatuetten des 16. Jahrhunderts,* Berlin, 1949.

MELLER, S. *Die deutschen Bronzestatuetten der Renaissance,* Munich, 1926.

Useful reviews of specific topics are supplied by:

MELLER, S. *Peter Vischer der Ältere und seine Werkstatt,* Leipzig, 1925.

TROESCHER, G. *Conrad Meit,* Freiburg, 1927.

OBERHAMMER, V. *Die Bronzestandbilder des Maximiliangrabmal in der Hofkirche zu Innsbruck,* Innsbruck, 1935.

BOHEMIA

OPITZ, J. *Gotische Plastik der 14. und 15. Jahrhunderts in Böhmen,* Kaaden, 1924.

THE NETHERLANDS

Except in general volumes, Early Netherlandish sculptors and sculpture have not been widely treated. They are usually treated by regions, and as with Germany, the Museum Catalogues are the basic source. The following are still useful:

CLEMENS, P. *Belgische Kunstdenkmäler,* Munich, 1923.

BOUDY, D.P.R.A. *Middeleeuwische Beeldhouwkunst,* Amsterdam, 1947.

ENGLAND

PRIOR, E. S. and GARDNER, A. *An Account of Medieval Figure-Sculpture in England,* Cambridge, 1921.

GARDNER, A. *English Medieval Sculpture,* Cambridge, 1951.

STONE, L. *Sculpture in Britain—The Middle Ages,* Harmondsworth, 1955.

ZARNECKI, G. *English Romanesque Sculpture 1066-1140,* London, 1951.

ZARNECKI, G. *Later English Romanesque Sculpture, 1140-1210,* London, 1953. Both in the Tiranti Series.

SAXL, F. *English Sculptures of the Twelfth Century,* London, 1954. Breaks the ground and represents the splendid work of the Warburg Institute in bringing a greater awareness of Early English art to England and the English-speaking world.

HARVEY, J. H. *Gothic England - A Survey of National Culture, 1300-1550,* London, 1947.

OAKESHOTT, W. *Classical Inspiration in Medieval Art,* London, 1959.

BOND, F. *Wood Carvings in English Churches, I Misericords, II Stalls and Tabernacle Work.* Oxford, 1910. 2 vols.

CAVE, C. J. P. *Roof Bosses in Medieval Churches,* Cambridge, 1948.

CROSSLEY, F. H. *English Church Monuments, 1150-1550,* London, 1921.

ANDERSON, M. D. *The Medieval Carver,* Cambridge, 1935.

ANDERSON, M. D. *Animal Carvings in British Churches,* Cambridge, 1938.

GARDNER, A. *Alabaster Tombs of the Pre-Reformation period in England,* Cambridge, 1940.

Among the volumes of the Oxford History of English Art:

BOASE, T. S. R. *English Art, 1100-1216,* Oxford, 1953.

EVANS, J. *English Art, 1307-1461,* Oxford, 1949.

SPAIN AND PORTUGAL

For medieval sculpture:

The volumes of the *Ars Hispaniae.*

GOMEZ-MORENO, M. *Breve Historia de la Escultura Española,* Madrid, 1951.

SANTOS, R. DOS. *A Escultura em Portugal,* Lisbon, 1948-50, 2 vols.

KINGSLEY PORTER, A. *Spanish Romanesque Sculpture,* Paris, 1928, 2 vols.

WEISE, G. *Spanische Plastik aus sieben Jahrhunderten,* Reutlingen, 1925-39. 4 vols. in 6.

For the sixteenth century:

GÓMEZ-MORENO, M. *The Golden Age of Spanish Sculpture,* London, 1964.

WEISE, G. *Die Spanische Plastik der Renaissance und des Frühbarock,* Tubingen, 1956.

ORUETA, R. de *Berruguete y su obra,* Madrid, 1917.

II Italian Sculpture

Italian Sculpture has been the focus of most study over the last century, with the result that the bibliography is much richer than that for other areas. Whereas in Germany and the North the most detailed research has been lavished on the catalogues of the great collections, and these are thus our primary sources, in Italy these catalogues hardly exist, and scholarship tends to find its outlet in outside books and papers. On grounds of accessibility, however, this bibliography has been confined to books.

GENERAL WORKS

CASTIGLIONE, B. *Il Cortigiano,* various editions both in Italian and English. The classic work on courtly behaviour and an important source-book for the philosophy of the early Cinquecento.

VASARI, G. *Le Vite...,* 2nd edition, Florence, 1568; standard critical edition edited by Milanesi, Florence, 1878-85. Many English language editions are available. The most important source of information concerning Italian artists up to *c.* 1565, and in particular the Florentines, by a man who was a distinguished artist himself and a personal friend of Michelangelo and Cosimo I.

BORGHINI, R. *Il Riposo,* Florence, 1584. Continues the story up to *c.* 1584, again with the main accent on Florence, revealing in its Counter - Reformation sentiments.

BAGLIONE, G. *Le Vite de' pittori, scultori, et architetti...,* Rome, 1642. Basic source for information on artists of the early Seicento, though highly biased in places - against Caravaggio, for instance.

BELLORI, G.P. *Le Vite de' pittori, scultori, et architetti moderni,* Rome, 1672. Less concerned with systematic history than with putting forward the case for classicism in the controversy with the Baroque, in particular with his 'Idea'.

BALDINUCCI, F. *Notizie de' professori del disegno da Cimabue in qua,* Florence, 1681-1728. Monumental work summing up all earlier published writings with additional material, but extremely difficult to use as without an index.

PASCOLI, L. *Vite de' pittori, scultori, et architetti moderni,* Rome, 1730-36. Valuable source-book for the Baroque sculptors, particularly in Rome.

TEMANZA, T. *Vite dei più celebri architetti, e scultori Veneziani,* Venice, 1778.

Basic source-book for information on the Venetian artists.

VENTURI, A. *Storia dell'Arte italiana*, IV '*La Scultura del Trecento e le sue Origini*', Milan, 1906; VI '*La Scultura del Quattrocento*', Milan, 1908; X, Parts 1, 2, and 3, '*La Scultura del Cinquecento*', Milan 1935-37; Very comprehensive but incomplete corpus of Italian art, with accounts of the periods and artists, lists of their works, and large numbers of illustrations; invaluable, but by no means infallible in its attributions — inevitable in a pioneer work.

ROMANESQUE

CRICHTON, G. H. *Romanesque Sculpture in Italy,* 1954. Useful handbook, easily read and well illustrated.

FRANCOVICH, G. de *Benedetto Antelami, Architetto e Scultore e l'Arte del suo tempo,* Florence, 1952. Massive, packed with data and well illustrated.

SALVINI, R. *Wiligelmo e le Origini della Scultura Romanica,* Milan, 1956. Useful, with plenty of excellent plates.

GOTHIC

POPE-HENNESSY, J. *Italian Gothic Sculpture,* London, 1955. Admirably lucid survey of the subject with excellent plates, and each sculptor supplied with a succinct summary of his documentation and a critical bibliography.

CRICHTON, G.H. and E.R. *Nicola Pisano and the Revival of Sculpture in Italy,* Cambridge, 1938. Useful and readable.

KELLER, H. *Giovanni Pisano,* Vienna, 1942. Standard work.

VALENTINER, R. *Tino di Camaino: a Sienese sculptor of the fourteenth century,* Paris, 1935. Standard monograph with a full account of the sculptor.

SCHLOSSER, J. *Leben und Meinungen des Florentinischen Bildners Lorenzo Ghiberti,* Basle, 1941. Profound study that analyses Ghiberti's position in the Quattrocento.

KRAUTHEIMER, R. *Lorenzo Ghiberti,* Princeton, 1956. Very detailed study with particular emphasis on Ghiberti's debt to classical sculpture.

SUPINO, I.B. *Jacopo della Quercia,* Bologna, 1926. Well illustrated, but later research has invalidated some of the conclusions.

PLANISCIG, L. *Venezianische Bildhauer der Renaissance,* Vienna, 1921. Earlier sections of this work supply a useful summary of Venetian Gothic sculpture.

RENAISSANCE

POPE-HENNESSY, J. *Italian Renaissance Sculpture,* London, 1958. An invaluable survey of 15th century sculpture with excellent illustrations, and each sculptor supplied with a summary of his documentation and a critical bibliography.

FABRICZY, C. VON *Filippo Brunelleschi: sein Leben und sein Werke,* Stuttgart, 1892. Standard work with the documentation including the early biography by Tuccio Manetti.

JANSON, H.W. *The Sculpture of Donatello,* Princeton, 1957. Fundamental work with excellent *catalogue raisonné* and plates.

MARQUAND, A. *Luca della Robbia,* Princeton, 1914. The standard work but somewhat inadequately illustrated; the plates can be augmented by those in PLANISCIG, L.: *Luca della Robbia,* Florence, 1948.

PLANISCIG, L. *Bernardo und Antonio Rossellino,* Vienna, 1942. Somewhat superficial but plenty of plates.

PLANISCIG, L. *Desiderio da Settignano,* Vienna, 1942. Useful critical text and well illustrated.

CARDELLINI, I. *Desiderio da Settignano,* Milan, 1962. Detailed introduction and *catalogue raisonné*, with excellent illustrations.

MARQUAND, A. *Andrea della Robbia,* Princeton, 1922. Standard and almost only work available.

MARQUAND, A. *Giovanni della Robbia,* Princeton, 1920. Standard and almost only work available.

PLANISCIG, L. *Andrea del Verrocchio,* Vienna, 1941. Useful and well illustrated.

SABATINI, A. *Antonio e Piero Pollajuolo,* Florence, 1944. Well written but poorly illustrated and should be read in conjunction with the plates of ORTOLANI, S.: *Il Pollajuolo,* Milan, 1948.

WELLER, A. *Francesco di Giorgio,* Chicago, 1943. An excellent monograph, with a thorough *catalogue raisonné.*

RICCI, C. *Il Tempio Malatestiano,* Milan/Rome, 1925. Well written and amply illustrated, invaluable for Agostino di Duccio, Matteo de' Pasti, and their circle.

HILL, G. *A Corpus of Italian Medals before Cellini,* Oxford, 1930. Fundamental study of the great Renaissance medallists before Cellini, including Pisanello and Matteo de' Pasti.

PLANISCIG, L. *Venezianische Bildhauer der Renaissance,* Vienna, 1921. Good pioneer surveys of Antonio Bregno, Antonio Rizzo, Pietro and Tullio Lombardo, among others.

PLANISCIG, L. *Andrea Riccio,* Vienna, 1927. Comprehensive handling of not only Riccio and his workshop, but also Bellano. Well illustrated.

PAOLETTI, P. *L'Architettura e la Scultura del Rinascimento in Venezia,* Venice, 1873. Invaluable for the documentation of the Venetian sculptors' activities.

POPE-HENNESSY, J. *Italian High Renaissance and Baroque Sculpture,* London, 1963. The High Renaissance and 'Mannerist' section centres on excellent analyses of Michelangelo and Giambologna with concise surveys of the various artforms, and each sculptor discussed is supplied with a summary of his documentation and a critical bibliography.

TOLNAY, C. DE *Michelangelo,* 5 vols, Princeton, 1947 - 60. Includes a vast Michelangelo bibliography.

WILES, B. *The Fountains of the Florentine Sculptors,* Cambridge, 1933.

CAMESASCA, E. *Tutta l'opera del Cellini,* Milan, 1955. Very brief but succinct text with many if small illustrations.

SYMONDS, J. A. *The Life of Benvenuto Cellini written by himself,* edited by John Pope - Hennessy, London, 1949. More important for the light it casts on life in Italy between *c.* 1520-50 than for the understanding of Cellini's work.

DHANENS, E. *Jean Boulogne: Giovanni Bologna Fiammingo,* Brussels, 1956. Fundamental work on the sculptor with heavy documentation and the earliest lives reprinted *in toto.*

BAROQUE AND ROCOCO

WITTKOWER, R. *Art and Architecture in Italy, 1600-1750,* Harmondsworth, 1958. Brilliantly concise summary of the art of the period with extensive sections devoted to the principal sculptors and admirable synopses of the activities of the lesser known sculptors.

DELOGU, G. *La Scultura italiana del Seicento e del Settecento,* Florence, 1932-1933.

POPE-HENNESSY, J. *Italian High Renaissance and Baroque Sculpture,* London, 1963.

RICCOBONI, A. *Roma nell'Arte. La scultura nell'evo moderno,* Rome, 1942. Good survey of sculpture in Rome.

VIGEZZI, S. *La scultura Lombarda nell'eta barocca,* Milan, 1930. Basic work on the period.

LO MONACO, I. DI *Pittori e scultori siciliani dal Seicento al primo Ottocento,* Palermo, 1940. Basic work on Sicilian Baroque sculpture.

ROSSO, L. *La Pittura e la Scultura del '700 a Torino,* Turin, 1934. Basic work for Piedmontese sculpture of the Settecento.

WITTKOWER, R. *Gian Lorenzo Bernini,* London, 1955. Excellent, sympathetic introduction to Bernini with many good plates.

FRANSOLET, M. *François Du Quesnoy, Sculpteur d'Urbain VIII,* Brussels, 1941. Standard but not entirely satisfactory monograph with poor stylistic analyses.

DOMARUS, K. VON *Pietro Bracci, Beiträge*

273

zur römischen Kunstgeschichte des XVIII Jahrhunderts. Strasbourg, 1915. Basic survey of Late Baroque and Rococo sculpture in Rome.

LANKHEIT, K. *Florentinische Barockplastik, 1670-1743,* Munich, 1962. One of the finest books ever written on a single period of sculpture, brilliant analytical text, meticulous and vast documentation, and lavish illustrations.

MELI, F. *Giacomo Serpotta,* Palermo, 1934. Only study of any significance available.

III The Beginnings of Modern Sculpture

FRANCE

BLUNT, A. *Art and Architecture in France 1500-1700,* Harmondsworth, 1953, provides the best survey of the 16th and 17th centuries.

DILKE, L. *French Architects and Sculptors in the 18th Century,* London, 1900. The only book on this subject in English.

FRACASTEL, P. *La Sculpture de Versailles,* Paris, 1930, is rather more specialized.

THIRION, H. *Les Adam et Clodion*, Paris, 1885.

ROSEROT, A. *Edmé Bouchardon*, Paris, 1910.

KELLER-DORIAN, G. *Antoine Coysevox,* Paris, 1920, 2 vols.

RÉAU, L. *Etienne-Maurice Falconet,* Paris, 1922, 2 vols.

FRANCASTEL, P. *Girardon,* Paris, 1928.

RÉAU, L. *Les Lemoyne,* Paris, 1927.

RÉAU, L. *J.-B. Pigalle,* Paris, 1950.

ALIBERT, F. *Pierre Puget,* Paris, 1930.

BRION, M. *Pierre Puget,* Paris, 1930.

DIGARD, M. *Jacques Sarrazin,* Paris, 1934.

ROSTRUP, H. *J.-A. Houdon (1741-1828),* Copenhagen, 1942.

RÉAU, L. *Houdon,* Paris, 1930.

GIACOMETTI, G. *Le Statuaire Jean-Antoine Houdon et son Époque (1741-1828),* n.p., 1918-19, 3 vols.

GERMANY AND EASTERN EUROPE

FEULNER, A. *Die Deutsche Plastik des Sechzehnten Jahrhunderts,* Munich, 1926. Basic work.

SAUERLANDT, M. *Die Deutsche Plastik des Achtzehnten Jahrhunderts,* Munich, 1926. Basic work.

SCHÖNBERGER, A. *Deutsche Plastik des Barock,* Königstein im Taunus, 1963. Brief but excellent survey in the Blauen Bücher series.

BOECK, W. *Joseph Anton Feuchtmayer,* Tübingen, 1948.

MICHALSKI, E. *Balthasar Permoser,* Frankfurt, 1927.

SCHÖNBERGER, A. *Ignaz Günther,* Munich, 1954.

TIETZE-CONRAT, E. *Österreichische Barockplastik,* Vienna, 1920, reviews Austrian Baroque sculpture.

BLAUENSTEINER, K. *Georg Raphael Donner,* Vienna, 1944.

GRIMSCHITZ, B. *Georg Raphael Donner,* Stuttgart, 1959.

DECKER, H. *Barockplastik in den Alpenländern,* Vienna, 1943.

Basic surveys of Hungarian and Bohemian Baroque sculpture are supplied by:

AGGHÁZY, M. *Barockplastik in Ungarn,* Budapest, 1959.

STECH, V.U. *Die Barockskulptur in Böhmen,* Prague, 1959.

BELGIUM AND HOLLAND

GERSON, H. and TER KUILE, E.H. *Art and Architecture in Belgium, 1600-1800,* Harmondsworth, 1960. A general study of Belgian Baroque sculpture.

ROUSSEAU, H. *La Sculpture aux XVIIe et XVIIIe siècles,* Brussels, 1911. With the above, the only satisfactory general survey.

The following monographs fill out the picture:

WILLAME, G. *Laurent Delvaux,* Brussels and Paris, 1914.

DEVIGNE, M. *Laurent Delvaux et ses Elèves,* Brussels and Paris, 1928.

LIBERTUS, BROTHER. *Lucas Faydherbe*, Antwerp, 1930.

GABRIELS, J. *Artus Quellien de oude*, Antwerp, 1930.

NOTTEN, M. VAN *Rombout Verhulst*, The Hague, 1907.

Holland is covered in some detail by:

NEURDENBURG, E. *De zeventiende eeuwsche dellbhouwkunst in de noordelijke Nederlanden*, Amsterdam, 1948.

FREMANTLE, K. *The Baroque Town Hall of Amsterdam*, Utrecht, 1959, is valuable.

SPAIN AND PORTUGAL

KUBLER, G. and SORIA, M. *Art and Architecture in Spain and Portugal and their American Dominions - 1500 to 1800*, Harmondsworth, 1959. The most convenient survey for the later centuries, but has not superseded:

PILLEMENT, G. *La Sculpture Baroque Espagnole*, Paris, 1945.

WEISBACH, W. *Spanish Baroque Art*, Cambridge, 1941.

Monographs on specific artists include:

HERNÁNDEZ DÍAZ, J. *Juan Martínez Montañés*, Seville, 1949.

WETHEY, H. E. *Alonso Cano*, n.p., 1955.

ENGLAND

GUNNIS, R. *Dictionary of British Sculptors 1660-1851*, London, 1953. The basic source of information. Each entry summarizes the bibliography available.

ESDAILE, K.A. *English Monumental Sculpture since the Renaissance*, London, 1927, and

ESDAILE, K. A. *English Church Monuments 1510-1840*, London, 1946, are still reliable.

WHINNEY, M. *Sculpture in Britain 1530-1830*, Harmondsworth, 1964.

Useful monographs include:

BELL, C. F. *Annals of Thomas Banks*, Cambridge, 1938.

FABER, H. *Caius Gabriel Cibber*, London, 1926.

CONSTABLE, W. G. *John Flaxman*, London, 1927.

GREEN, D. *Grinling Gibbons, His Work as Carver and Statuary 1648-1721*, London, 1964.

SMITH, J. T. *Nollekens and His Times*, London, 1829.

ESDAILE, K. A. *Life of Roubiliac*, Oxford, 1928.

WEBB, M. I. *Michael Rysbrack, Sculptor*, London, 1954.

The Nineteenth Century

The basic problem of the bibliography of the 19th century is that while the stylistic developments are essentially international, the literature is almost entirely on a national basis. The following attempt to survey the century from an international viewpoint but with a strong bias towards the German areas:

BAUMGART, F. *Geschichte der abendländischen Plastik*, Cologne, 1956.

KUHN, A. *Die neuere Plastik von 1800 bis zur Gegenwart*, Munich, 1922.

NOVOTNY, F. *Painting and Sculpture in Europe 1780-1880*, Harmondsworth, 1960.

ENGLAND

GUNNIS, R. *Dictionary of British Sculptors 1660-1851*, London, 1953 covers sculptors up to 1851. After this date reliance mostly has to be placed on contemporary biographies and reviews, and the occasional article.

BELGIUM AND HOLLAND

DAALEN, P. K. VAN *Nederlandse beeldhouwers in de negentiende eeuw, Utrechtse bijfragen tot de Kunstgeshiedenis*, Utrecht, 1957.

FRANCE

BÜRGER-THORÉ, W. *Französische Kunst im*

neunzehnten Jahrhundert. Leipzig, 1911, 3 vols.

GERMANY

OSTEN, GERT VON DER *Plastik des 19. Jahrhunderts in Deutschland, Österreich und der Schweiz,* Königstein im Taunus, 1961.

SPAIN

WALDMANN, E. *Arte del realismo e impressionismo en el siglo XIX,* Barcelona, 1944.

ITALY

VIGEZZI, S. *La Scultura italiana dell'ottocento,* Milan, 1932.

MARCHIORI, G. *Scultura italiana dell'ottocento,* Verona, 1960.

Most important are the monographs on individual sculptors:

MUÑOZ, A. *Antonio Canova: Le Opere,* Rome, 1957.

CLÉMEN-CARPEAUX, L. *La vérité sur l'œuvre et la vie de J.-B. Carpeaux.* Paris, 1934-1935.

KAMPHAUSEN, A. *Asmus Jakob Carstens,* Neumünster i. Holstein, 1941.

DREYFOUS, M. *Dalou, sa vie et son œuvre,* Paris, 1903.

QUARRÉ, P. *La Vie et l'œuvre de François Rude,* (Musée de Dijon), Dijon, 1947.

MACKOWSKY, H. *Johann Gottfried Schadow: Jugend und Aufstieg 1764-1797,* Berlin, 1927.

SCHADOW, G. *Kunstwerke und Kunstansichten,* Berlin, 1849.

RAVE, P.O. *Thorvaldsen,* Berlin, 1944.

List of Illustrations

Introduction

1 Central doorpost, Beaulieu. French.

2 Base of a niche on the West Façade, Amiens Cathedral. French.

3 Adam Krafft (c. 1430-1507): Supporting figure, Sebaldskirche, Nuremberg. German.

4 Jean Goujon (died 1560s): Caryatid. Louvre, Paris. French.

5 M.B. Braun (1684-1738): Supporting figures. Clam-Gallas Palace, Prague. German.

6 Jacob Epstein (1880 - 1959): Supporting figures designed for the British Medical Association Building (now Rhodesia House), London. English.

7 Head of Christ. Capital. Nave of the Church of St Martin, Plaimpied. French.

8 Head of Christ. West Porch, Ulm Cathedral. German.

9 Michelangelo (1475 - 1564) : *Pietà* (detail). Florence Cathedral. Italian.

10 Gregorio Fernández (c. 1566-1636): Entombment (detail). National Museum of Sculpture, Valladolid. Spanish.

11 Joseph Wilton (1722-1803): Monument to General Wolfe. Westminster Abbey, London. English.

12 Effigy of a Knight. Dorchester Abbey, Oxfordshire. English.

13 Monument to the Prince-Bishop Dieter von Isenburg, Mainz Cathedral. German.

14 Monument to the Prince-Bishop Franz von Ingelheim, Mainz Cathedral. German.

I Medieval Sculpture in the North

15 The Adoration of the Magi. Probably English. Victoria and Albert Museum, London.

16 Carving (detail). Church at Urnes, Norway. Scandinavian.

17 Adam and Eve, detail from the West Door, Monreale Cathedral. Western European.

18 Crucifix of San Isidoro. Western European. Museo Aqueologico, Madrid.

19 Christ in Majesty, Tympanum of St Foy, Conques. French.

20 Last Judgment (detail). Tympanum of St Foy, Conques. French.

21 St Andrew. Cloister of St Pierre, Moissac. French.

22 The Prophet Isaiah. Abbey Church of Souillac. French.

23 St John the Baptist (detail), Chartres Cathedral. French.

24 Doorpost, St Pierre, Moissac. French.

25 Doorpost, Abbey Church of Souillac. French.

26 Samson and the Lion, capital, Anzy-le-Duc. French.

27 Hunter Roundel. Dado of the Church of St Gilles. French.

28 Head of a Tau Cross. English. Victoria and Albert Museum, London.

29 Capital, formerly Church of St Sernin, Toulouse. French. Musée des Augustins, Toulouse.

30 The Last Judgment (detail). The tympanum of Autun Cathedral. French.

31 A Prophet. Detail of West Porch, Avallon. French.

32 West Porch (detail). St Trophime, Arles. French.

33 The Raising of Lazarus, Chichester Cathedral. English.

34 The Apostles. Malmesbury Abbey, Wiltshire. English.

35 The Choir Screen (detail). Bamberg Cathedral. German.

36 Detail of a frieze. Church of St Gilles. French.

37 Wilgelmus (active 11-12th c.): Scenes from the Creation, West Façade, Modena Cathedral. Italian.

38 B. Antellami (active late 12th c.): *December*. Labours of the Month. Baptistery of S. Giovanni, Parma. Italian.

39 The Third Mode of Music. Capital. Formerly Abbey Church of Cluny. French. Cluny Museum, Paris.

40 Capitals, Wells Cathedral. English.

41 West façade of the tower, Temple of Parasurameswar. Indian.

42 Tympanum, Church of St Pierre, Moissac. French.

43 Tympanum, Shobden Church, Herefordshire. English.

44 Two Prophets, Charlieu Abbey. French.

45 Old Testament Figures. West Porch. Chartres Cathedral. French.

46 Christ Blessing. South Porch, Chartres Cathedral. French.

47 St John, formerly St Mary's Abbey, York. English. The Yorkshire Museum, York.

48 Coronation of the Virgin. East Tympanum, South Porch. Strasbourg Cathedral. French.

49 Procession of Canons. South Porch, Amiens Cathedral. French.

50 The Visitation. Central Porch, Rheims Cathedral. French.

51 Signs of the Zodiac. West Front, Amiens Cathedral. French.

52 The Virgin and Child. Louvre, Paris. French.

53 Foliage capitals. The Chapter House, Southwell Minster. English.

54 Centaur and Dragon. Roof boss, Muniments Room, Westminster Abbey, London. English.

55 Draughtspiece. Possibly English. Victoria and Albert Museum, London.

56 Eckehart and Uta, Choir, Naumburg Cathedral. German.

57 Timo von Kistritz, Choir, Naumburg Cathedral. German.

58 The 'Bamberg Rider', Bamberg Cathedral. German.

59 The Soissons Diptych. Said to have been formerly in the Cathedral at Soissons. French. Victoria and Albert Museum, London.

60 The Attack on the Castle of Love on a mirror-case. French or possibly German. Victoria and Albert Museum, London.

61 The Virgin and Child. French. The Victoria and Albert Museum, London.

62 The Deposition. French. Louvre, Paris.

63 Madonna of the Rosebush. German. Bayerisches Nationalmuseum, Munich.

64 Effigy of Henry III. Westminster Abbey, London. English.

65 Detail of the Effigy of Richard II, Westminster Abbey, London. English.

66 Detail of the Effigy of Edward III, Westminster Abbey, London. English.

67 Detail of the tomb of Aymer de Valance, Westminster Abbey, London. English.

68 Tomb of Jean sans Peur. Franco-Flemish, Musée des Beaux Arts, Dijon, France.

69 St Catherine in Prison. English. Victoria and Albert Museum, London.

70 Detail of Altarpiece from Oplinter. Flemish.

71 The Flagellation. Detail of Altarpiece formerly in the Collegiate Church of Lircy, near Troyes. French. Victoria and Albert Museum, London.

72 Claus Sluter (1360-1406): Detail of Angel from the *Puits de Moïse*, Chartreuse, Dijon. French.

73 Madonna and Child. French. Musée des Augustins, Toulouse.

74 *Pietà.* South German. Bayerisches Nationalmuseum, Munich.

75 Madonna and Child. German. Fürstenfeldbruck, Germany.

76 St Peter. West façade, Regensburg Cathedral. German.

77 Hans Multscher (1427 - 1467) : St George and St John the Evangelist. West Porch, Ulm Cathedral. German.

78 Michael Pacher (*c.* 1435-1498): Detail of St Michael. German. Bayerisches Nationalmuseum, Munich.

79 Figure of a Saint. Hal Cathedral, Belgium. Flemish.

80 *Pietà.* German. Rheinisches Landesmuseum, Bonn.

81 Michael Pacher (*c.* 1435-1498): Detail from the St Wolfgang Altar, St Wolfgang, Austria. German.

82 Veit Stoss (?1447-1533): The Virgin and Child. German. Victoria and Albert Museum, London.

83 Nicolas Gerhardt (active 15th century): Virgin and Child with St Anne. German. Deutsches Museum, Berlin.

84 Virgin and Child from Dangolsheim (? Simon Lainberger). German. Deutsches Museum, Berlin.

85 Tilman Riemenschneider (1460-1531): Detail of limewood group. Greglingen a. Tauber. German.

86 Riemenschneider: Detail of group of the Holy Kindred. German. Victoria and Albert Museum.

87 Mourning over the Dead Christ. French.

88 Conrad Meit (d. 1550/1) : Tomb of Philibert le Beau, Brou, France. German.

89 Peter Vischer (1454 - 1529) : Hercules. Detail of the Shrine of St Sebald, Sebaldskirche, Nuremberg. German.

90 Vischer: Shrine of St Sebald, Sebaldskirche, Nuremberg. German.

91 Conrad Meit (d. 1550/1): *Judith.* German. Bayerisches Nationalmuseum, Munich.

92 Boxwood Medallion. German. Victoria and Albert Museum, London.

93 A. Daucher (d. 1523/4): Christ with Mary and St John, Fugger Chapel, Church of St Anne, Augsburg. German.

94 Master H. L. (active between 1515-1530): Altarpiece, Breisach. German.

II Italian Sculpture

95 Giovanni Pisano (active *c.* 1275 - after 1314): Haggai (fragment of figure). Victoria and Albert Museum, London.

96 Nicola Pisano (active 1258-78): Relief of the Crucifixion. Pulpit, Baptistery, Pisa.

97 Nicola Pisano: *Fidelity.* Pulpit. Baptistery, Pisa.

98 Giovanni Pisano (active *c.* 1275 - after 1314): A Deacon. Pulpit, S. Andrea, Pistoia.

99 Tino di Camaino (active before 1311, d. 1337): Monument of Mary of Valois. S. Chiara, Naples.

100 Nino Pisano (*c.* 1315 - ? 1368): Angel of the Annunciation. Victoria and Albert Museum, London.

101 Giovanni Pisano (active *c.* 1275 - after 1314): A Prophet. Fontana Maggiore, Perugia.

102 Tino di Camaino (active before 1311, d. 1337): *Charity*, detail of the Monument to Catherine of Austria, S. Lorenzo Maggiore, Naples.

103 Nino Pisano (*c.* 1315 - ? 1368): *Madonna del Latte.* S. Maria della Spina, Pisa.

104 Lorenzo Maitani (*c.* 1275 - 1330): Detail of the relief of *Scenes from Genesis.* Main façade of Orvieto Cathedral.

105 Arnolfo di Cambio (active 1265 -
? 1302): *Frieze of Mourning Acolytes*. Cloister of S. Giovanni in
Laterano, Rome.

106 Andrea Orcagno (active 1344-68):
Relief of *The Burial of the Virgin*,
Orsanmichele, Florence.

107 Donatello (1386-1466): Relief of
Dancing Children. External Pulpit
of the Cathedral, Prato.

108 Lorenzo Ghiberti (1378-1455): Relief of *The Sacrifice of Isaac*, Bargello (Museo Nazionale), Florence.

109 Filippo Brunelleschi (1377 - 1446):
Relief of *The Sacrifice of Isaac*.
Bargello, Florence.

110 Donatello (1386 - 1466) : *David*.
Bargello, Florence.

111 Donatello: *Zuccone*. Museo del-
l'Opera del Duomo, Florence.

112 Luca della Robbia (1400 - 1482):
Relief of *Trumpeters and Dancing
Children*. Cantoria, Museo del-
l'Opera del Duomo, Florence.

113 Donatello (1386 - 1466): Relief of
St George and the Dragon. Beneath
the tabernacle of the Arte dei Co-
razzi, Orsanmichele, Florence.

114 Bernardo Rossellino (1409 - 1460):
Tomb of Leonardo Bruni. S. Croce,
Florence.

115 Bernardo Rossellino: Madonna and
Child tondo from the Bruni Tomb,
S. Croce, Florence.

116 Donatello: (1386-1466): *The Pazzi
Madonna*. Staatliche Museum, Berlin.

117 Desiderio da Settignano (1428-1464):
Head of an Angel. Altar of the Sacrament, S. Lorenzo, Florence.

118 Andrea Arditti: Reliquary bust of
St Zenobias. Cathedral Treasury,
Florence.

119 Antonio Rossellino (1427 - c. 1479):
Portrait bust of Giovanni Chellini.
Victoria and Albert Museum, Lon-
don.

120 Andrea della Robbia (1435 - 1525):
Altarpiece of the *Agony in the Garden*. Louvre, Paris.

121 Lorenzo Ghiberti (1378-1455): Four
panels from the North Door of the
Baptistery, Florence.

122 Andrea Pisano (c. 1290-1348): Four
panels from the North Door of the
Baptistery, Florence.

123 Lorenzo Ghiberti (1378-1455): Detail of panel of the North Door of
the Baptistery, Florence.

124 Ghiberti: Relief of *The Story of
Cain and Abel*. Panel from the
East Door of the Baptistery, Florence.

125 Benedetto da Maiano (1442-1497):
Relief of *The Stigmatization of St
Francis*. Pulpit in S. Croce, Flo-
rence.

126 Lorenzo Ghiberti (1378-1455): *St
Matthew*. In the tabernacle of the
Arte del Cambio, Orsanmichele, Flo-
rence.

127 Jacopo della Quercia (c. 1374-1438):
Tomb of Ilaria del Carretto, Lucca
Cathedral.

128 Della Quercia: Detail of the Trenta
Altar, S. Frediano, Lucca.

129 Della Quercia: Relief of *Zacharias
in the Temple*. Font of the Baptistery, Siena.

130 Della Quercia: Relief of *The Creation of Adam*. Detail of Porta
Maggiore, S. Petronio, Bologna.

131 Niccolò dell'Arca (c. 1435 - 1494) :
Prophet wearing a turban, Arca di
S. Domenico, S. Domenico, Bologna.

132 Guido Mazzoni (active after 1473,
d. 1518): Detail of *tableau vivant*
of *The Lamentation over the Dead
Christ*. S. Giovanni Battista, Modena.

133 Donatello (1386-1466): *The Virgin
and Child Enthroned*, High Altar of
the Santo, Padua.

134 Donatello: Relief of *The Miracle
of the Unbeliever's Mule*. High Altar of the Santo, Padua.

135 Donatello: Relief of *The Entomb ment*. Back of the High Altar of the Santo, Padua.

136 Bartolommeo Bellano (*c.* 1434-1496/ 1497): *Europa and the Bull*. Bargello, Florence.

137 Riccio (*c.* 1470/5-1532): *Mounted Warrior*. Victoria and Albert Museum, London.

138 Il Antico (*c.* 1460?-1528): *Meleager*. Victoria and Albert Museum, London.

139 Cristoforo Mantegazza (active 1464, d. 1482) or Antonio Mantegazza (active before 1473, d. 1495): *A Prophet*. Façade of the Certosa, Pavia.

140 Venetian Gothic School (? Giovanni Buon, *c.* 1355 - after 1428): High relief of *The Fall*. Palazzo Ducale, Venice.

141 Antonia Rizzo (active after 1465, d. 1499/1500): *Eve*. Palazzo Ducale, Venice.

142 Tullio Lombardo (*c.* 1455 - 1532): *Bacchus and Ariadne*. Kunsthistorisches Museum, Vienna.

143 Donatello (1386-1466): *Lamentation over the Dead Christ*. Victoria and Albert Museum, London.

144 Francesco di Giorgio (1439-1501/2): Relief of *The Flagellation*. Galleria Nazionale dell'Umbria, Perugia.

145 Agostino di Duccio (1418 - 1481): Relief of *An Angel drawing back a Curtain*. Tempio Malatestiano, Rimini.

146 Agostino di Duccio: Relief of *A Miracle of S. Bernardino*. Oratory of S. Bernardino, Perugia.

147 Francesco Laurana (*c.* 1430 - ? 1502): High relief of *Alphonso of Aragon in Triumph* (detail). Castelnuovo, Naples.

148 Bertoldo di Giovanni (*c.* 1420-1491): *Arion*. Bargello, Florence.

149 Antonio Pollaiuolo (1431/2-1498): *Hercules and Antaeus*. Bargello, Florence.

150 Pollaiuolo: Tomb of Sixtus IV. Grotte Vaticane, St Peter's, Rome.

151 Andrea del Verrocchio (1435-1488): *Christ and Doubting Thomas*. Orsanmichele, Florence.

152 Benedetto da Maiano (1442-1497): *St Sebastian*. Misericordia, Florence.

153 Michelangelo (1475-1564): *Angel bearing a Candlestick*, Arca di San Domenico Maggiore, San Domenico Maggiore, Bologna.

154 Michelangelo: *The Bruges Madonna*. Notre Dame, Bruges.

155 Michelangelo: *Ignudo*. Detail of the ceiling of the Sistine Chapel, Rome.

156 Jacopo Sansovino (1486-1570): *Apollo*. Loggetta, Piazza San Marco, Venice.

157 Sansovino: *Neptune*. Palazzo Ducale, Venice.

158 Michelangelo (1475-1564): *The Dying Slave*. Louvre, Paris.

159 Riccio (*c.* 1470/75-1532): Relief of *The Death of Della Torre*. Louvre, Paris.

160 Rosso Fiorentino (1495 - 1540) : *Ignudo*. Galerie François I, Fontainbleau.

161 Benvenuto Cellini (1500-1571): *The Nymph of Fontainbleau*. Louvre, Paris.

162 Niccolò Tribolo (1500-1550): Fountain of Hercules and Antaeus. Villa Castello, near Florence.

163 Pierino da Vinci (1520/1 or 1531-1554): *Putto*. Detail from the Fountain of Antaeus, Villa Castello, near Florence.

164 Vincenzo Danti (1530-1576): Relief of *Moses and the Brazen Serpent*. Bargello, Florence.

165 Michelangelo (1475-1564): *Pietà*. Florence Cathedral.

166 Benvenuto Cellini (1500-1571): *Perseus*. Loggia de' Lanzi, Florence.

167 Cellini: Pedestal of the *Perseus*. Loggia de' Lanzi, Florence.

168 Bartolommeo Ammanati (1511-1592): *Marine Goddess.* Fountain of Neptune, Piazza della Signoria, Florence.

169 Pietro Francavilla (1548 ? - 1615): *Winter.* Ponte Santa Trinità, Florence.

170 Giambologna (1529-1608): *Neptune.* Fountain of Neptune, Piazza del Nettuno, Bologna.

171 Giambologna: *The Rape of the Sabine.* Loggia de' Lanzi, Florence.

172 Giambologna: *Hercules and the Centaur.* Loggia de' Lanzi, Florence.

173 Danese Cattaneo (*c.* 1509 - 1573): *Fortuna.* Bargello, Florence.

174 Alessandro Vittoria (1525 - 1608): *Neptune with Sea Horse.* Victoria and Albert Museum, London.

175 Niccolò Roccatagliata (active 1593-1636): *Bacchus.* Victoria and Albert Museum, London.

176 Giambologna (1529 - 1608): *Marching Soldiers.* Detail of relief, pedestal of equestrian monument to Cosimo I. Piazza della Signoria, Florence.

177 Camillo Mariani (1565?-1611): *St Catherine.* San Bernardo alle Terme, Rome.

178 Francesco Mocchi (1580-1654): *Angel of the Annunciation.* Museo dell'Opera del Duomo, Orvieto.

179 Mocchi: Equestrian monument to Ranuccio Farnese, Piazza Cavalli, Piacenza.

180 Mocchi: Detail of the relief of the *Allegory of Good Government* on the base of the monument to Ranuccio Farnese, Piazza Cavalli, Florence.

181 Gianlorenzo Bernini (1598 - 1680): *St Theresa.* Cornano Chapel, S. Maria della Vittoria, Rome.

182 Bernini: *Rape of Proserpine.* Galleria Borghese, Rome.

183 Bernini: *Apollo and Daphne.* Galleria Borghese, Rome.

184 Bernini: *David.* Galleria Borghese, Rome.

185 Bernini: The Baldacchino and Cathedra Petri. St Peter's, Rome.

186 Bernini: *St Longinus.* St Peter's, Rome.

187 François Duquesnoy (1594 - 1643): *St Andrew.* St Peter's, Rome.

188 Gianlorenzo Bernini (1598 - 1680): *The River Nile.* Fountain of the Four Rivers, Piazza Navona, Rome.

189 François Duquesnoy (1594 - 1643): *S. Susanna.* S. Maria di Loreto, Rome.

190 Alessandro Algardi (1595 - 1654): Relief of *The Meeting of Leo I and Attila.* St Peter's, Rome.

191 Pietro da Cortona (1596-1669): Decorative stuccoes. Detail of the Sala di Giove, Palazzo Pitti, Florence.

192 Gianlorenzo Bernini (1598 - 1680): Tomb of Urban VIII. St Peter's, Rome.

193 Bernini: Tomb of Alexander VII. St Peter's, Rome.

194 Melchiorre Caffà (1635 - 1667/8): Relief of *The Ecstasy of St Catherine.* S. Caterina da Siena, Monte Magnanapoli, Rome.

195 Ercole Ferrata (1610-1686): Relief of *The Stoning of St Emerenziana.* Detail. S. Agnese in Piazza Navona, Rome.

196 Antonio Raggi (1624-1686): Allegorical figures. Detail of Clerestory of Nave of the Gesù, Rome.

197 Filippo Carcani (entered the Accademia di San Luca 1678): Decorative figures. Detail of semi-dome, Capella Lancellotti, S. Giovanni in Laterano, Rome.

198 Camillo Rusconi (1658-1728): *St Matthew.* S. Giovanni in Laterano, Rome.

199 Pietro Bracci (1700-1773): *Neptune.* Detail of the Fontana Trevi, Rome.

200 Filippo della Valle (1697 - 1700): *Temperance.* Capella Corsini, S. Giovanni in Laterano, Rome.

201 Giambattista Foggini (1652-1737): Bust of Cardinal Gian Carlo de' Medici. Victoria and Albert Museum, London.

202 Foggini: *The Flaying of Marsyas.* Private Collection, Great Britain.

203 Giacomo Serpotta (1656-1732): *Charity.* Oratory of San Lorenzo, Palermo.

204 Luigi Vanvitelli (1700-1773): Groups of *Diana and Actaeon.* Great Cascade, Caserta.

205 Antonio Corradini (1668 - 1752): *Modesty.* Capella Sansevero de' Sangri, Naples.

206 Francesco Queirolo (1704 - 1762): *Deception.* Capella Sansevero de' Sangri, Naples.

207 Raffaele Monti (1818-1881): *Veiled Woman.* The Wallace Collection, London.

III The Beginnings of Modern Sculpture

208 Pietro Torrigiano (1472-1528): Detail from the Monument to Henry VII, Westminster Abbey, London. Italian work in England.

209 Torrigiano: Detail from the Monument to Henry VII, Westminster Abbey, London. Italian work in England.

210 Domenico del Barbiere, called Domenico Fiorentino (1506-1565/75): *Charity.* S. Pantaleon, Troyes. Italian work in France.

211 St John the Baptist. S. Pantaleon, Troyes. French.

212 Germain Pilon (1535?-1590): Caryatids for the urn which contained the heart of Henri II. French. Louvre, Paris.

213 Jean Goujon (d. in the 1560s): Monument to Louis de Brézé, Rouen. French.

214 Goujon: Two nymphs from the *Fontaine des Innocents.* French. Louvre, Paris.

215 Goujon (under Primaticcio): Stucco decorations, Fontainebleau. French.

216 Germain Pilon (1535?-1590): Cadavers from the monument to Henri II and Catherine dei Medici. St Denis, near Paris. French. Photograph from a cast.

217 Pilon: Cadaver from the monument to Valentine Balbiani. French. Louvre, Paris.

218 Pilon: *The Deposition.* French. Louvre, Paris.

219 Pilon: *The Virgin.* French. Louvre, Paris.

220 Pilon: Detail of the kneeling figure of René de Birague. French. Louvre, Paris.

221 Michel Anguier (1612-1686): *Ceres.* French. Victoria and Albert Museum, London.

222 Pierre Puget (1622-1694): *Milo of Crotona.* French. Louvre, Paris.

223 Cornelis Floris (1540-1570): *Christ carrying the Cross.* Tournai Cathedral, Belgium. Flemish.

224 Mantelpiece, Town Hall, Antwerp. Flemish.

225 Bernard Strauss (active 2nd half of the 17th c.) Tankard. German (Augsburg). Victoria and Albert Museum, London.

226 Leonhard Kern (1588-1663): *Diana.* German. Victoria and Albert Museum, London.

227 Jörg Zurn (1583 - c. 1630): Detail of the Virgin Mary. Annunciation group. High Altar of the Church of Überlingen. German.

228 Jörg Petel (1601 - c. 1634): *Venus and Cupid.* German. Ashmolean Museum, Oxford.

229 Hans Krumper (1586-1647): *Justice.* Residenz, Munich. German.

230 Nicolas Stone (1586-1647): Monument to John Donne, St Paul's Cathedral, London. English.

231 Monument to the St John family, Lydiard Tregoze, Wilts. English.

232 Siloe Workshop: Monument to Don Garcia Osorio. Spanish. Victoria and Albert Museum, London.

233 Pompeo Leoni (c. 1533-1608): *Philip II.* Spanish. Prado Museum, Madrid.

234 Juan de Juní (c. 1507-1577): *The Entombment.* Spanish. National Museum of Religious Carvings, Valladolid.

235 Pedro de Mena (1656-1704): *Mary Magdalene.* Spanish. National Museum of Sculpture, Valladolid.

236 Pedro de Mena (1656-1704): *A Boy Saint.* Private collection, Barcelona. Spanish.

237 Pedro de Mena (1656-1704): *The Virgin of Sorrows.* Spanish. Victoria and Albert Museum, London.

238 Luisa Roldán (1656-1704): *The Virgin of the Macerena.* Seville. Spanish.

239 Antoine Coysevox (1640-1720): *Mercury,* Tuileries Gardens, Paris. French.

240 Gaspard (c. 1624-1681) and Balthasar (1620-1674) Marsy: Fountain of Latona, Versailles. French.

241 Antoine Coysevox (1640-1720): Bust of Lebrun. French. Wallace Collection, London.

242 Edmé Bouchardon (1698-1762): *Love Cutting his Bow.* French. Louvre, Paris.

243 J. H. Fragonard (1732-1806): Detail of panel painting, 'The Meeting', from a room in the Frick Collection, New York. French.

244 Etienne Falconet (1716-1791): *Bathing Girl.* French. Louvre, Paris.

245 Claude Michel, called Clodion (1738-1810): *Cupid and Psyche.* French. Victoria and Albert Museum, London.

246 J. A. Houdon (1741-1828): Bust of Madame Victoire. French. Wallace Collection, London.

247 Willem de Groff (1680-1742): *Prince Maximilian von Bayern.* German. Altoetting, Bavaria.

248 Luc Faid'herbe (1617-1692): Monument to the Berthout family. Church of St Rombout, Malines, Belgium. Flemish.

249 H. F. Verbruggen (1655-1724): *Adam and Eve.* Detail of pulpit, Cathedral of St Gudule, Brussels. Flemish.

250 Ignaz Günther (1725-1775): *Apostles.* Detail. Chapel of Schloss Sünching, near Regensburg. German.

251 J. B. Neumann (1687-1735) and others: Interior of the Church of Vierzehnheiligen. German.

252 Balthasar Permoser (1651-1732): Supporting Figures. The Zwinger, Dresden. German.

253 Ignaz Günther (1725-1775): Male Saint. Rott-am-Inn, Bavaria. German.

254 Franz Josef Holzinger (1691?-1775). Stucco group, High Altar, Altenburg. Austrian.

255 G. R. Donner (1693-1741): *Providence.* Austrian.

256 F. X. Messerschmidt (1736-1783): *Character head.* Austrian. Victoria and Albert Museum, London.

257 Edward Pierce (d. 1695): Bust of Sir Christopher Wren. English. Ashmolean Museum, Oxford.

258 J. Bushnell (d. 1700): *Sir Thomas Gresham.* The Old Bailey, London. English.

259 L. F. Roubiliac (1705-1762): Monument to the Duke of Argyle. South Transept, Westminster Abbey, London. English.

260 J. M. Rysbrack (1694-1770): Monument to Sir John Dutton. Sherborne, Dorset. English.

261 Joseph Nollekens (1737-1823): *The Countess of Yarborough.* Mausoleum at Brocklesby Park, Lincolnshire. English.

262 Joseph Wilton (1722-1803): Bust of Oliver Cromwell. English. Victoria and Albert Museum, London.

263 John Bacon (1740-1799): Monument to Sir William Blackstone. All Soul's College, Oxford. English.

264 Sir Richard Westmacott (1775-1856): Negro from the monument to Charles James Fox. Westminster Abbey, London. English.

265 Joseph Nollekens (1737-1823): Monument to Sir Thomas and Lady Salusbury. Great Offley Church, Hertfordshire. English.

266 Antonio Canova (1757-1822): *Theseus and the Minotaur*. Italian. Victoria and Albert Museum, London.

267 Barthel Thorwaldsen (1770-1844): *Shepherd-Boy*. Danish. Thorwaldsen Museum, Copenhagen.

268 Johann Gottfried Schadow (1764-1850): *The Princesses Luise and Frederika of Prussia*. German. Staatliche Museen, Berlin.

269 John Gibson (1790-1866): *The 'Tinted Venus'*. English. Collection P. J. Dearden.

270 Samuel Joseph (1791-1850): Monument to Wilberforce. Westminster Abbey, London. English.

271 François Rude (1784-1855): *The Imperial Eagle watching over Napoleon*. French. Musée des Beaux Arts, Dijon.

272 J. B. Carpeaux (1827-1875): *Dancer with Tambourine*. French. Private Collection, London.

273 Jules Dalou (1838-1902): *A Woman Reading*. French. Victoria and Albert Museum, London.

274 Alfred Stevens (1817-1875): *Virtue overcoming Vice*. English. Tate Gallery, London.

275 Vincenzo Gemito (1852-1922): *The Fisherboy*. Italian. Museo Nazionale, Florence.

276 Auguste Rodin (1840-1917): *The Muse*. French. The Tate Gallery, London.

Acknowledgments for Photographs

A. C. L., Brussels: 70, 224, 248, 249. Alinari, Florence: 96, 102, 105, 106, 108, 109, 110, 112, 113, 114, 118, 124, 125, 127, 128, 129, 130, 131, 132, 133, 135, 136, 141, 144, 145, 146, 148, 149, 150, 151, 152, 153, 154, 155, 156, 162, 164, 165, 166, 167, 170, 171, 172, 178, 179, 183, 184, 185, 186, 187, 190, 191, 193, 195, 196, 197, 198, 200, 203, 205, 206, 218, 275. Anderson, Rome: 97, 99, 103, 126, 147, 181. Archives Photographiques, Paris: 160, 244. Ashmolean Museum, Oxford: 257. Lala Aufsberg, Sonthofen/Aufsberg: 32, 89, 90, 239. Author's Archives: 19, 20, 21, 22, 79, 223. Brogi: 98, 111, 117, 121, 122, 134, 199. Cabinetto Fotografico Nazionale, Rome: 177, 189, 194. Peter Cannon Brookes: 1, 2, 3, 5, 8, 17, 26, 31, 36, 37, 44, 48, 49, 63, 72, 75, 76, 77, 78, 91, 101, 104, 107, 120, 125, 139, 140, 157, 158, 163, 168, 169, 176, 180, 188, 204, 210, 211, 212, 219, 229, 240, 253, 254. C. J. P. Cave: 54. A. C. Cooper, London: 272. *Country Life,* London: 231. Courtauld Institute of Art: 30, 40, 230, 258, 260, 263. Flammarion, Paris: 87. Fox Photos, London: 247. Frick Collection, New York: 243. Giraudon, Paris: 4, 24, 25, 27, 29, 39, 42, 51, 68, 73, 88, 159, 161, 213, 214, 215, 216, 217, 220, 222. Helga Schmidt Glassner: 56, 58. Hirmer Verlag, Munich: 250. F. L. Kenett: 9, 10, 59, 61, 62, 65, 66, 74, 80, 83, 84, 86, 209, 234, 235, 236, 274, 276. A. F. Kersting, London: 34. Kunsthistorisches Museum, Vienna: 142, 173. Eugen Kusch, Schwarzenbruck: 227. M. Lang: 93. Lincoln City Library, Museum and Art Gallery: 261. Louvre, Paris: 242. Marburg, Marburg/Lahn: 13, 14, 23, 35, 45, 50, 94, 251, 252. MAS, Barcelona: 18. Prado, Madrid: 233. Pierre Rambach: 41. Royal Commission on Historical Monuments: 33, 43, 64, 67, 265, 270. G. Schaffert, Greglingen: 85. Edwin Smith: 12, 53. Staatliche Museen, Berlin: 116, 268. Thames and Hudson Archives: 7, 16, 38. Thorwaldsen Museum: 267. Vatican Museum Archives: 192. Victoria and Albert Museum: 15, 28, 69, 71, 82, 92, 95, 100, 119, 137, 138, 143, 174, 175, 201, 202, 221, 225, 226, 232, 237, 245, 256, 262, 266, 269, 273. Wallace Collection: 207, 241, 246. Warburg Institute: 11, 208, 259. Hans Wild: 6.

Index of Names

Numbers in italics indicate plates

Adam, L. S., 240, 241
Adam, Robert, 259
Alberti, 105, 148
Albizzi, Rinaldo degli, 146
Algardi, Alessandro, *190*, 179, 181, 182, 187,
  188, 189, 193, 211
Amadeo, Giovanni, 134
Ammanati, Bartolommeo, *168*, 165, 220
Angelico, Fra, 123
Anguier, François, 211
Anguier, Michel, *221*, 211
Antellami, B., *38*, 34
Antico, Il, *138*, 134, 156
Arditti, Andrea, *118*, 116
Arca, Niccolò dell', *131*, 127
Arnold of Brescia, 23
Asam brothers, 249, 251
Aspetti, Tiziano, 169

Bacon, John, *263*, 256, 258
Bandinelli, Baccio, 161
Begarelli, Antonio, 127
Bellano, Bartolommeo, *136*, 130, 132, 134
Bellini, Giovanni, 128
Bellini, Jacopo, 132
Bernini, Gianlorenzo, *181*, *182*, *183*, *184*,
  185, *186*, *188*, *192*, *193*, 174, 177-86, 187,
  188, 189, 190, 194, 224, 232, 236, 240
Bernini, Pietro, 170, 171, 177
Bernward, 19
Boizot, Simon-Louis, 242
Bologna, Giovanni, 212, 216, 220
Bontemps, Pierre, 206-7
Bouchardon, Edmé, *242*, 238, 241
Bracci, Pietro, *199*, 190, 193
Braun, M. B., *5*, 11
Bregno, Andrea, 134
Brunelleschi, Filippo, *109*, 109, 110, 112
Bruni, Leonardo, 114
Buon, Giovanni, *140*
Bushnell, J., *258*, 253

Caffà, Melchiorre, *194*, 187-8, 189
Calcagni, Tiberti, *165*
Camaino, Timo di, *99*, *102*, 98, 102
Cambio, Arnolfo di, *105*, 98, 102
Cano, Alonso, 229
Canova, Antonio, *266*, 260, 261
Caravaggio, Michelangelo da, 171
Carcani, Filippo, *197*, 187, 188, 189
Carpeaux, J. B., *272*, 268
Carracci, Annibale, 171, 177
Castagno, Andrea del, 138
Castiglione, Baldassare, 151-2
Cattaneo, Danese, 168
Cellini, Benvenuto, *161*, *166*, *167*, 159-60,
  164, 168, 198, 206

Chantrey, Sir Francis, 258
Cheere, Sir Henry, 254, 258
Clodion, *245*, 232, 241-2
Coeck, Pieter, 214
Colt family, 217, 222
Cordieri, Nicolo, 170, 171
Corradini, Antonio, *205*, 187, 193, 194
Cortona, Pietro da, *191*, 179, 181, 184, 211
Coustou, Guillaume I, 235
Coysevox, Antoine, *239*, *241*, 235
Cure family, 217, 222

Dalou, Jules, *273*, 268
Danti, Vincenzo, *164*, 162
Daucher, Adolf, 94, 95
Delcour, Jean, 244
Delvaux, Laurent, 243, 255
Desjardins, Martin, 235, 243
Dietz, Ferdinand, 248, 251
Dolci, Carlo, 230
Donatello, *107*, *110*, *111*, *113*, *116*, *133*, *134*,
  135, *143*, 109, 110-14, 118, 123, 128-32,
  134, 138-40, 142, 144
Donner, Rafael, *255*, 252
Duccio, Agostino di, *145*, *146*, 140
Duquesnoy, François, *187*, *189*, 179-81, 186,
  218, 244

Egell, Paul, 251
Epstein, Jacob, *6*, 12, 264
Evesham, Epiphanius, 224

Faid'herbe, Luc, *248*, 244
Falconet, Étienne, *244*, 240, 241
Fanelli, Francesco, 224
Farnese, Cardinal Odoardo, 171
Feichtmayr, Joseph-Anton, 251
Fernández, Gregorio, *10*, 226
Ferrata, Ercole, *195*, 187, 188-9, 191
Ficino, Marsilio, 146, 148, 150, 152
Fiesole, Mina da, 115, 140
Fiorentino, Domenico, *210*, 199
Fiorentino, Rosso, *160*, 139, 157, 158, 159,
  160, 206
Flaxman, John, 258, 260
Floris, Cornelis, *223*, 214
Foggini, Giambattista, *201*, *202*, 187, 191, 193
Fragonard, J. H., *243*, 241
Francavilla, Pietro, *169*, 165
François I, 158, 205, 206, 207
Froissart, Philippe, 60, 61

Gaulli, Giovanni Battista, 184, 185, 188
Gemito, Vincenzo, *275*, 268
Gerhardt, Hubert, 217, 220
Gerhardt, Nicolas, *83*, 85

Ghiberti, Lorenzo, *108, 121, 123, 124, 126,* 109-10, 118, 120, 123, 124, 152
Giambologna, *170, 171, 172, 176,* 164, 165-8, 191
Gibbons, Grinling, 243, 246, 254
Gibson, John, *269,* 262
Giorgio, Francesco di, *144*
Giovanni, Bertoldo di, *148,* 139, 144, 147
Girardon, François, *235, 237*
Giselbert, 46
Godescharle, Gilles Lambert, 246
Goujon, Jean, *4, 213, 214, 215,* 206-7, 239
Green family, 253
Groff, Willem de, *247,* 243
Guelfi, Antonio, 256
Guillan, Simon, 211
Günther, Ignaz, *250, 253,* 241, 248, 251

Hagenauer, Johann Baptist, 252
H. L., Master, 95
Holleman family, 222
Holzinger, Franz Josef, *254*
Houdon, Jean Antoine, *246,* 242, 260

Jorhan family, 251
Joseph, Samuel, *270*
Juní, Juan de, *234,* 226

Kaendler, Johann Joachim, 253
Kern, Leonhard, *226*
Keyser, Hendrik de, 218, 224
Kistritz, Timo von, *57, 59*
Krafft, Adam, *3,* 11
Kristeller, P. O., 148
Krumper, Hans, *229,* 220

Lainberger, Simon, *84, 85,* 251
Laurana, Francesco, *147,* 142
Lebrun, Charles, *233, 237*
Lefebeure, 235
Legros, Alphonse, 239
Lehongre, Etienne, 235
Lemoyne, J. B., *235,* 241
Leoni, Pompeo, *233,* 208, 225, 226
Lesueur, Hubert, 224
Lippi, Filippino, 115
Lombardo, Pietro, 137
Lombardo, Tullio, *142,* 137, 156
Lücke family, von, 253

Maiano, Benedetto da, *125, 152,* 123, 142, 145
Maitani, Lorenzo, *104,* 104
Mantegazza, Cristoforo and Antonio, *139,* 134
Mantegna, Andrea, 128, 132, 137
Maratta, Carlo, 185, 189
Mariani, Camillo, *177,* 171
Marin, Joseph-Charles, 232, *234,* 242
Marshall family, 224
Marsuppini, Carlo, 115
Marsy, Gaspard and Balthasar, *240*
Masaccio, 112, 128

Mazarin, Cardinal, 205
Mazza, Giuseppe, 187, 193
Mazzonia, Guido, *132,* 127
Medici, Catherine dei, 205
Medici, Cosimo de', 108, 140, 146, 160, 168
Medici, Lorenzo de', 108, 146, 147
Meit, Conrad, *88, 91,* 90, 91
Mena, Pedro de, *235, 236, 237,* 227
Messerschmidt, F. X., *256,* 233, 252
Messina, Antonella da, 128
Michelangelo, *9, 153, 154, 155, 158, 165,* 127, 148, 149, 150, 152, 153-7, 158, 160, 163, 168, 178, 198
Michelozzo, Michelozzi, 113, 142
Mignard, Pierre, 237
Millan, Pedro, 226
Mirandola, Pico della, 146, 151-2
Mocchi, Francesco, *178, 179, 180,* 171, 172, 177
Moll, Balthazar, 252
Monaco, Lorenzo, 120-3
Monnot, P. E., 239
Montáñez, Martínez, 227
Monti, Raffaele, *207,* 194
Montorsoli, Giovanni, 160
Mora, José de, 227
Mostaert, Nicolas, 170
Multscher, Hans, *77, 82*

Neumann, J. B., *251*
Nollekens, Joseph, *261, 265,* 243, 256, 261
Nost family, 254

Opstal, Gérard van, 243
Orcagna, Andrea, *106,* 104

Pacher, Michael, *78, 81,* 84
Pajou, Augustin, 241
Parmigianino, Francesco, 150, 157
Parodi, Filippo, 187
Permoser, Balthasar, *252,* 11, 248, 255
Petel, Jörg, *228,* 220
Pierce, Edward, *257,* 253
Pigalle, J. B., 241
Pilon, Germain, *212, 216, 217, 218, 219, 220,* 207-11, 239
Pisano, Andrea, *122,* 98, 102, 118
Pisano, Giovanni, *95, 98, 101,* 98, 99, 102, 104
Pisano, Nicola, *96, 97,* 98, 99, 102
Pisano, Nino, *100, 103,* 98, 102, 104
Pollaiuolo, Antonio, *149, 150,* 145
Pontormo, Jacopo, 139
Poussin, Nicolas, 179, 186
Power, Hiram, 262
Prieur, Barthelmy, 211
Primaticcio, Francesco, *215,* 159, 160, 206, 208
Puget, Pierre, *222,* 212, 236

Queirolo, Francesco, *206,* 194
Quellin family, 243, 244

Quellinus, Artus, 218
Quellinus, Artus II, 244
Quercia, Jacopo della, *127, 128, 129, 130,* 124-7, 140

Raggi, Antonio, *196,* 187, 188, 189
Raphael, 46, 109, 148, 150, 152, 156, 157
Reynolds, Joshua, 230
Riccio, Il, *137, 159,* 131, 132, 134, 157, 169
Riechle, Hans, 220
Riemenschneider, Tilman, *85, 86,* 86, 251
Rigaud, Hyacinthe, 191
Rixueno, 229
Rizzo, Antonio, *141,* 134
Robbia, Andrea della, *120*
Robbia, Luca della, *112,* 85, 113, 117-8
Roccatagliata, Niccolò, *175,* 169
Rodin, Auguste, *276,* 264, 265, 268
Roldán, Luisa, *238,* 229
Roldán, Pedro, 229
Romano, Giulio, 157
Rossellini, Antonio, *119,* 116, 142
Rossellino, Bernardo, *114, 115,* 85, 114-5
Roubiliac, Louis François, *259,* 255-6
Rubens, Peter Paul, 175, 181, 197, 217, 242
Rude, François, *271,* 210, 264, 268
Rusconi, Camillo, *198,* 187, 189-90, 193
Rysbrack, Michael, *260,* 243, 255

Sacchi, Andrea, 179, 185
St Non, 259
Salvi, Nicola, 190
Sansovino, Andrea, 123, 150, 156
Sansovino, Jacopo, *156, 157,* 156, 158, 168, 198
Sarrazin, Jacques, 211
Sarto, Andrea del, 158
Sassoferrato, 230
Savonarola, 109
Schadow, Johann Gottfried, *268,* 260
Schardt, Johann Gregor v. der, 220
Scheemaker family, 243, 255
Schluter family, 248
Serpotta, Giacomo, *203,* 187, 194
Settignano, Desiderio da, *117,* 115
Sforza family, 147
Siloe, The, *232,* 226

Slodz, Sebastian, 235
Sluter, Claus, *72,* 79, 127
Soldani, Massimiliano, 187, 191, 193
Stanton family, 253
Stevens, Alfred, *274*
Stone, Nicholas, *230,* 224
Stoss, Veit, *82,* 84-5
Straub, J. B., 251
Strauss, Bernard, *225*
Susini, Antonio, 165

Tacca, Pietro, 165
Taylor, Henry Osborne, 60
Taylor, Sir Robert, 254
Thorwaldsen, Barthel, *267,* 260
Torrigiano, Pietro, *208, 209,* 198, 225
Tribolo, Niccolò, *162,* 160
Tuby, Jean-Baptiste, 235

Valle, Filippo della, *200,* 190, 193
Van Cleve, 235, 243
Van Dyck, 175, 181, 217
Van Gelder, 243, 255
Vanvitelli, Luigi, *204,* 194
Vasari, Giorgio, *165,* 150, 152, 161
Vecchietta, 140
Veneziano, Domenico, 128
Verbruggen, H. F. *249,* 245
Verhaegen, Theodor, 245
Verhulst, Rombout, 245
Verrochio, Andrea del, *151,* 130, 145, 147
Vinci, Leonardo da, 147-50
Vinci, Pierino da, *163*
Vischer, Peter, *89, 90,* 91
Visconti, Gian Galeazzo, 106
Vittoria, Alessandro, *174,* 168
Vliete, Gillis van den, 170
Vries, Adrien de, 217, 220

Warin, Jean, 211
Westmacott, Sir Richard, *264,* 258
Wilgelmus, *37,* 33
Wilton, Joseph, *11, 262,* 256
Winckelmann, Johann Joachim, 259

Xavery family, 246

Zurn, Jörg, *227,* 220